Responsable d'Alfa

ADULTE COLORIAGE LIVRE PACK EDITION

Coloring Bandit

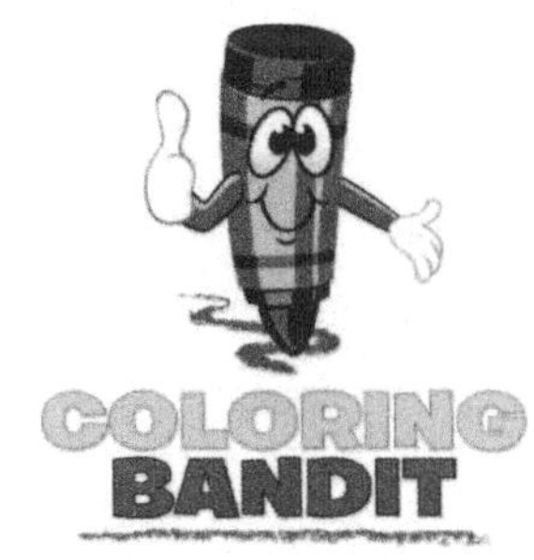

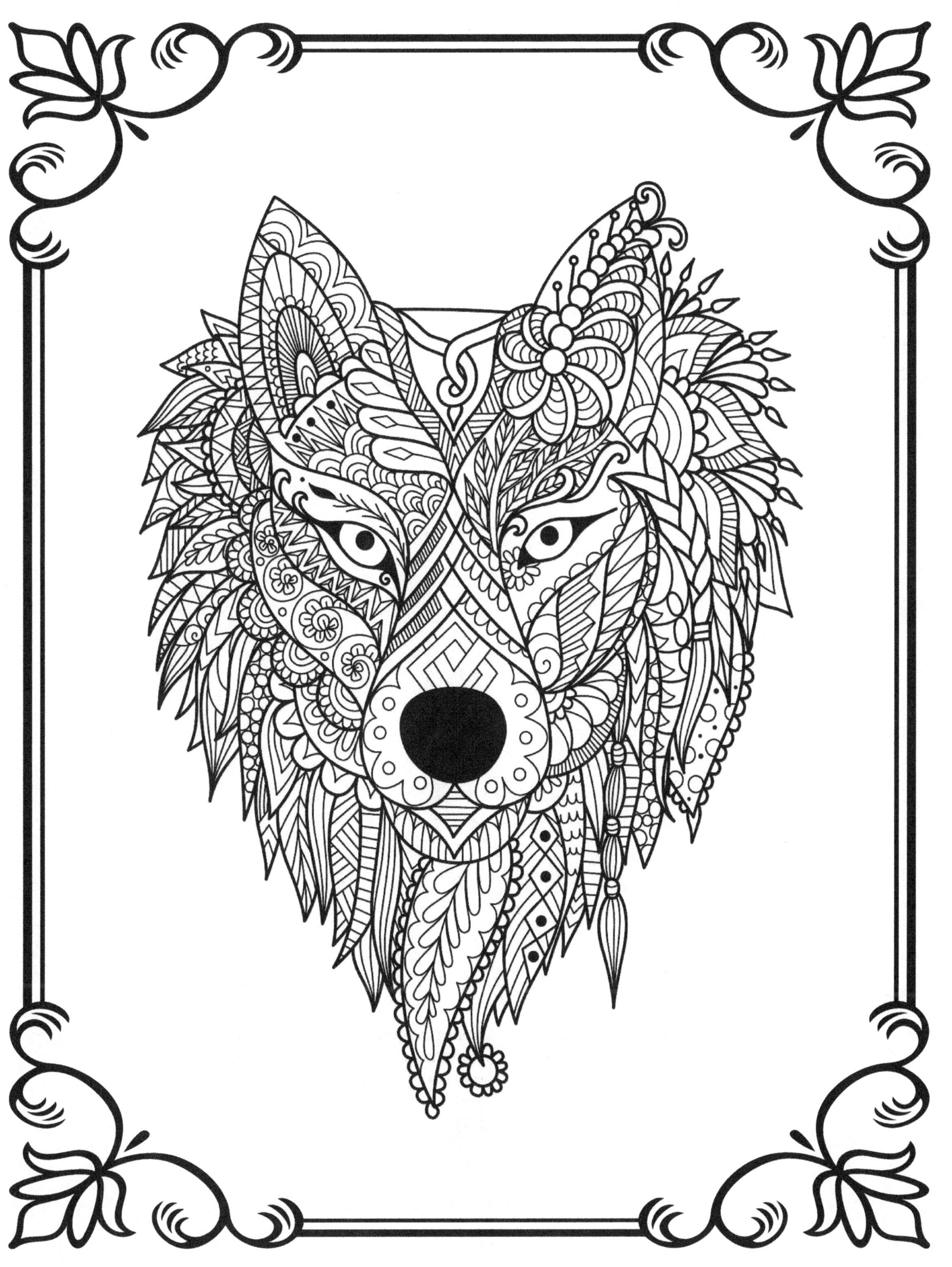

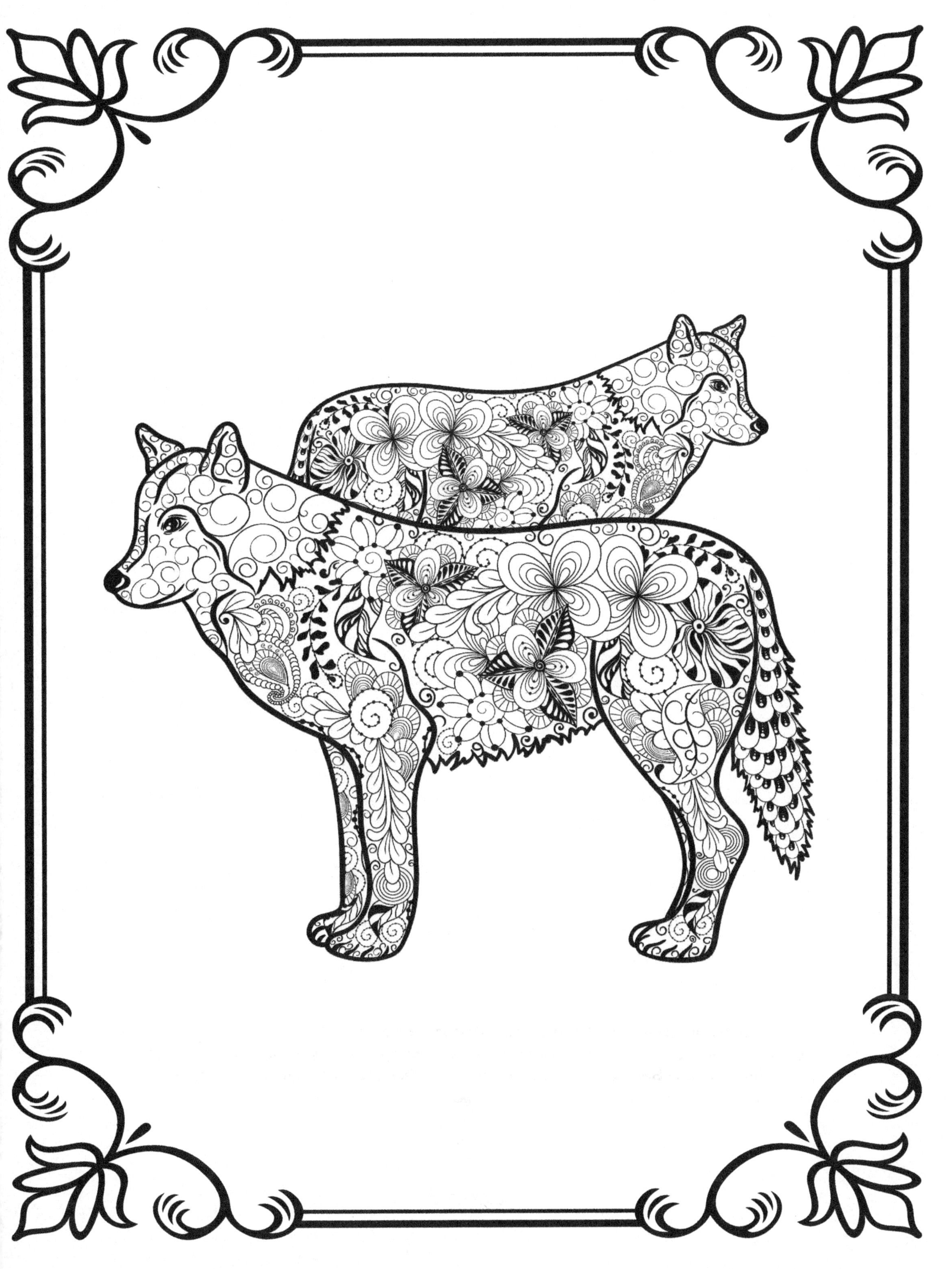

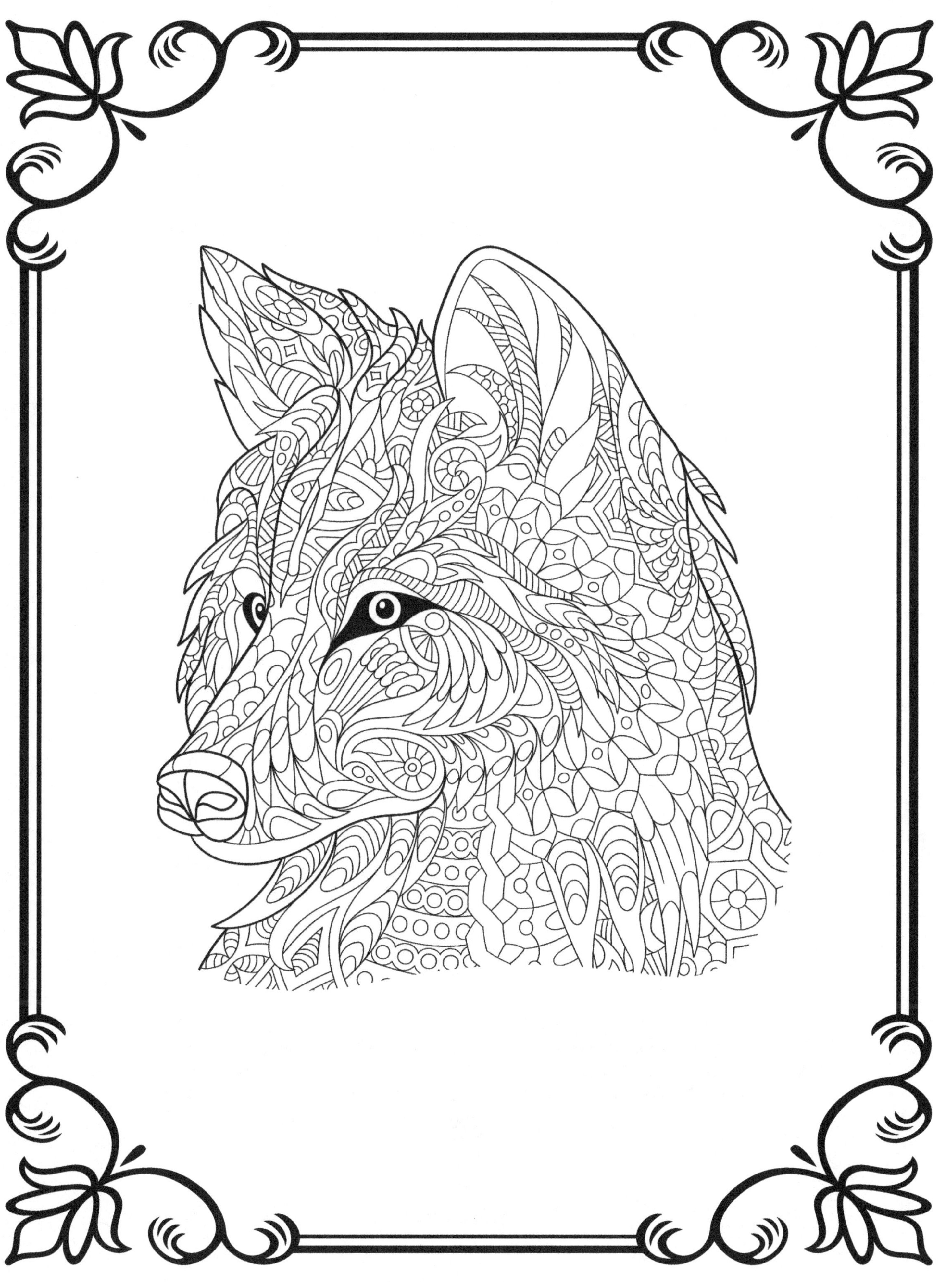

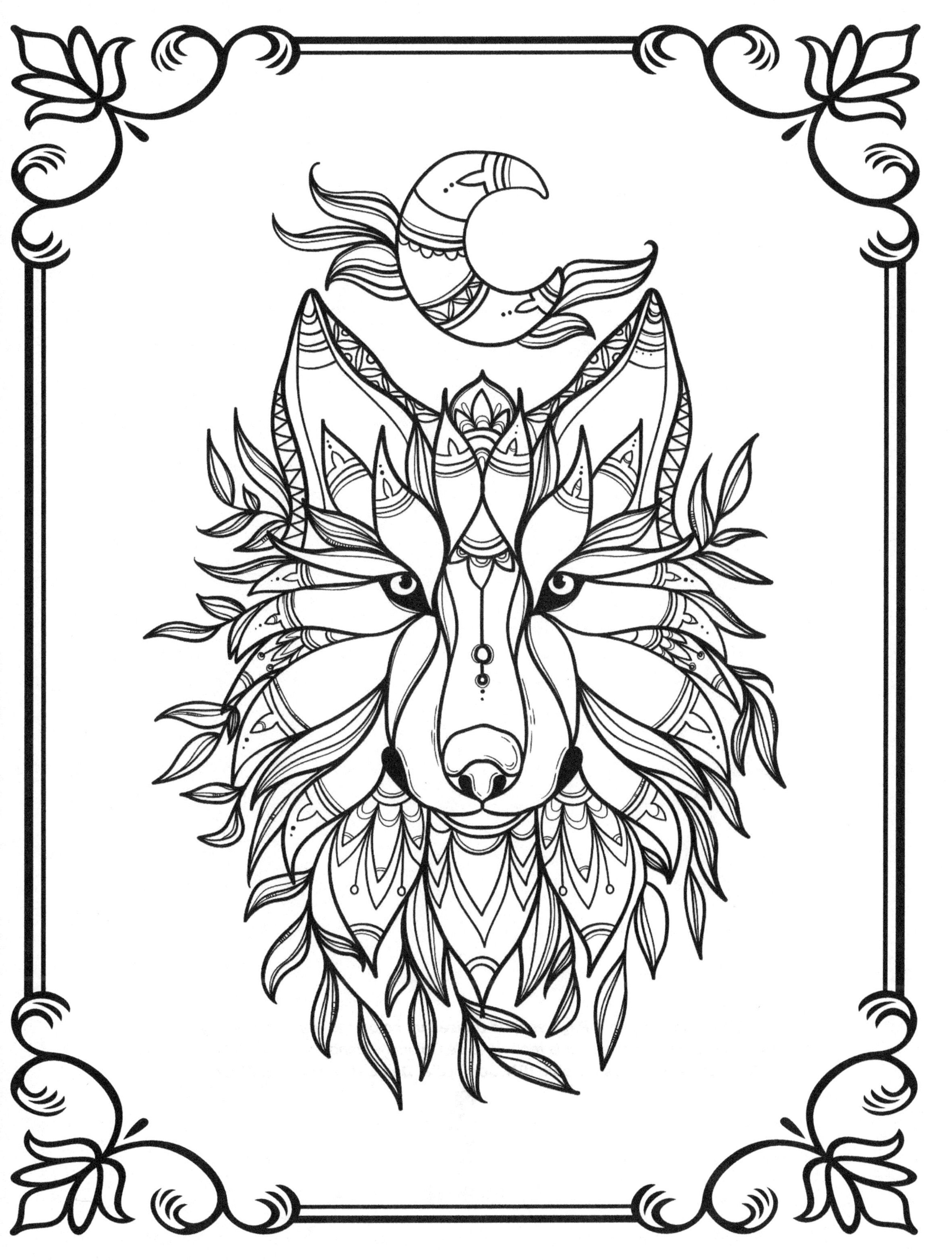

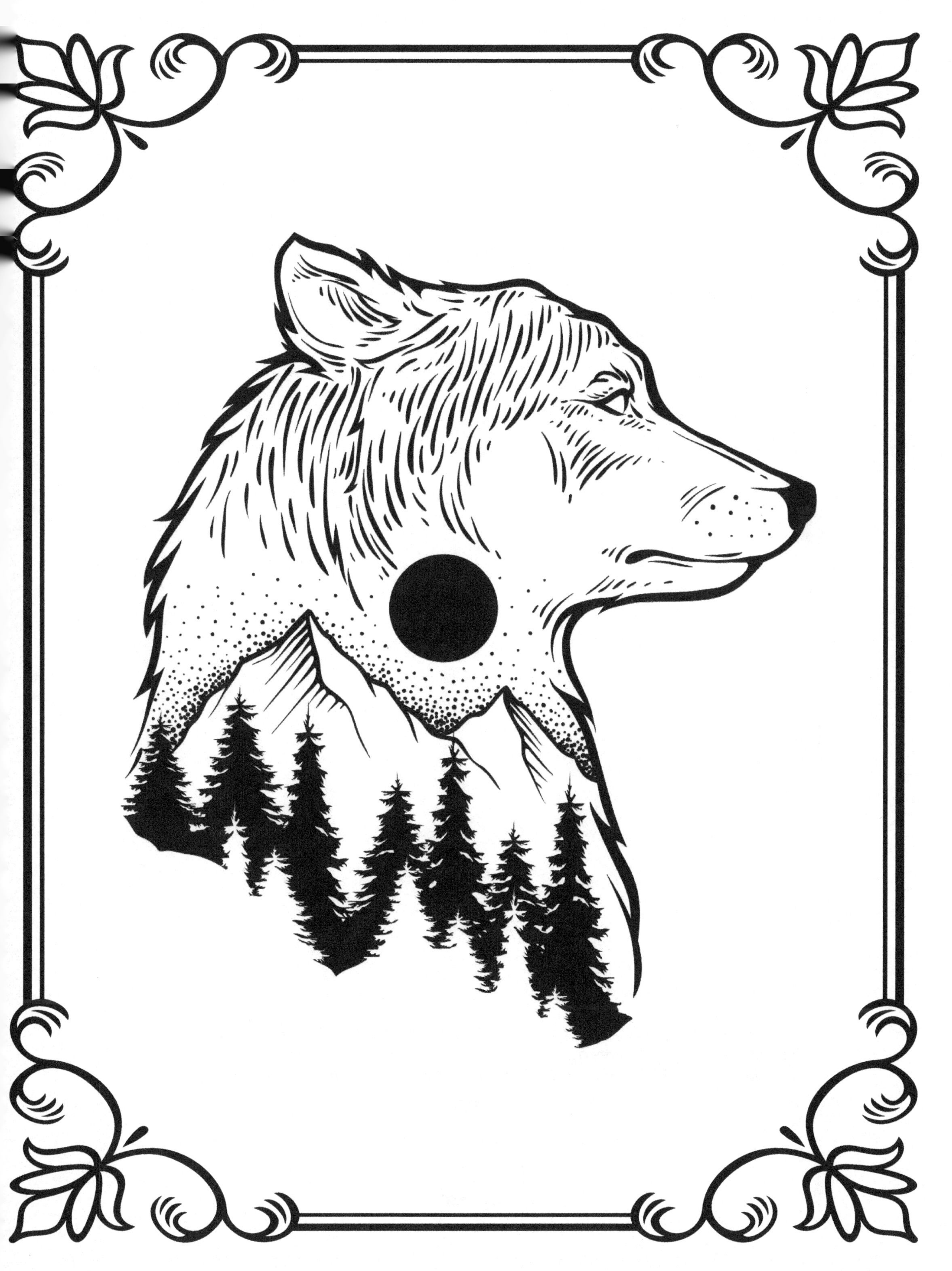

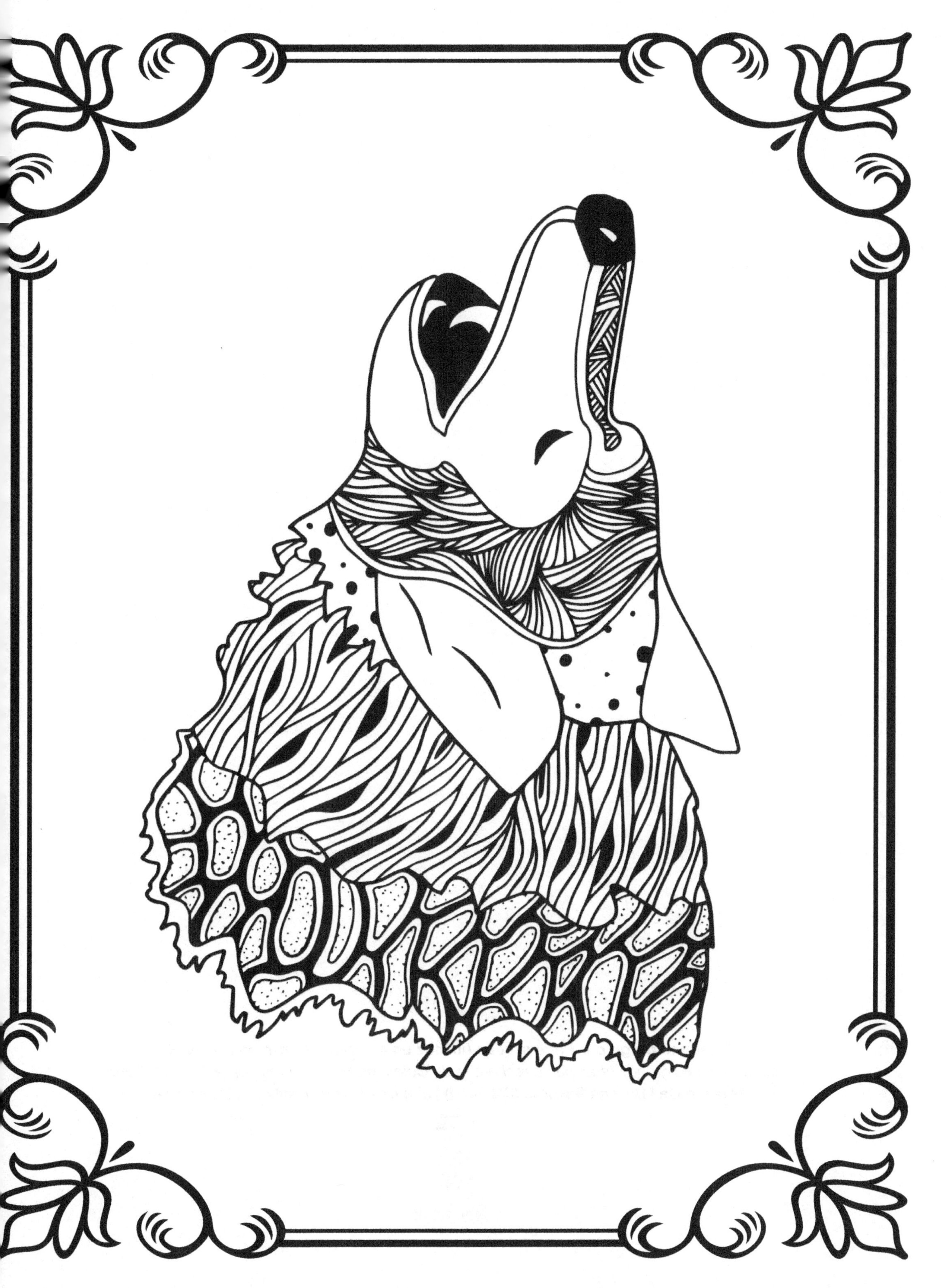

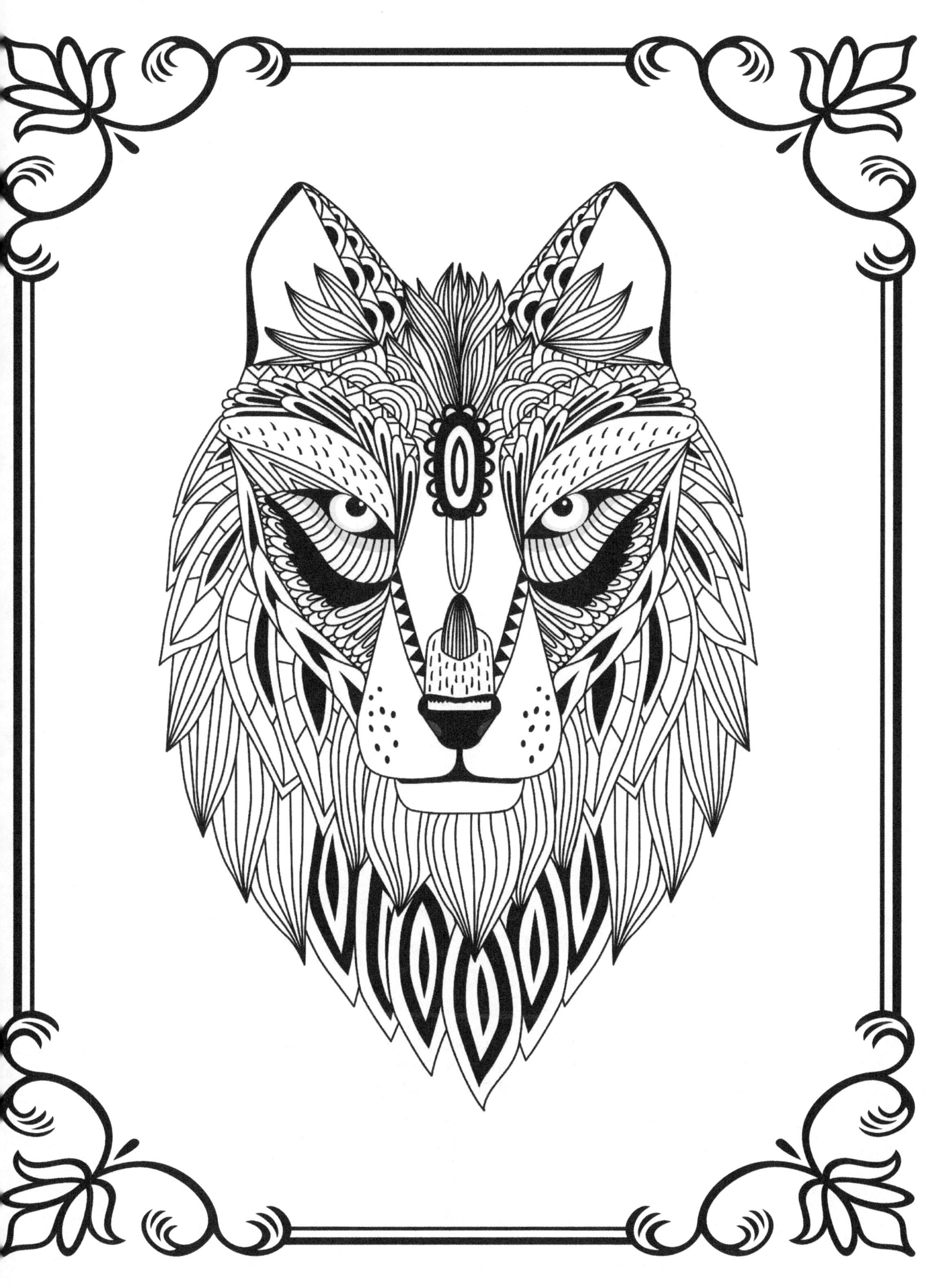

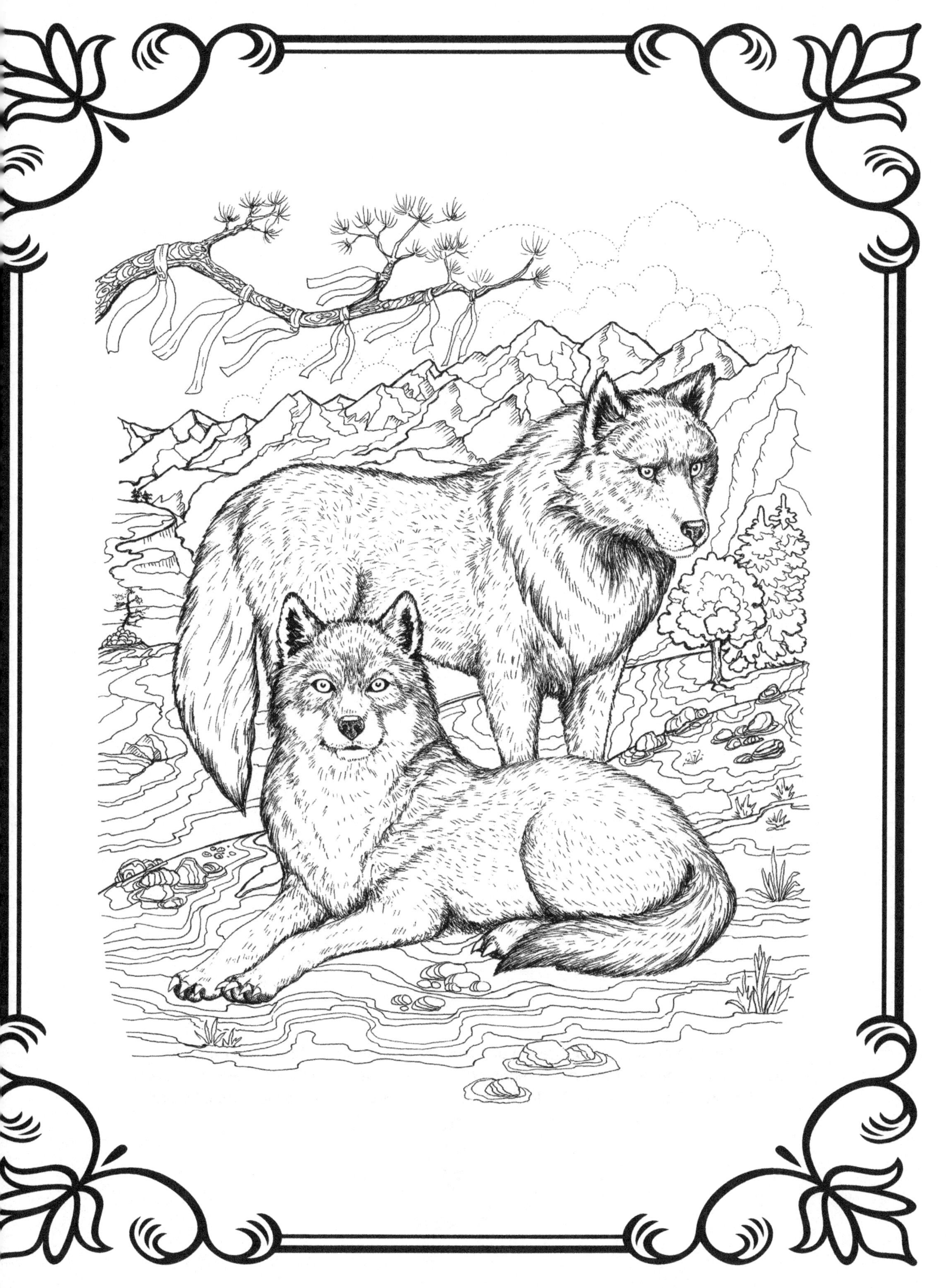

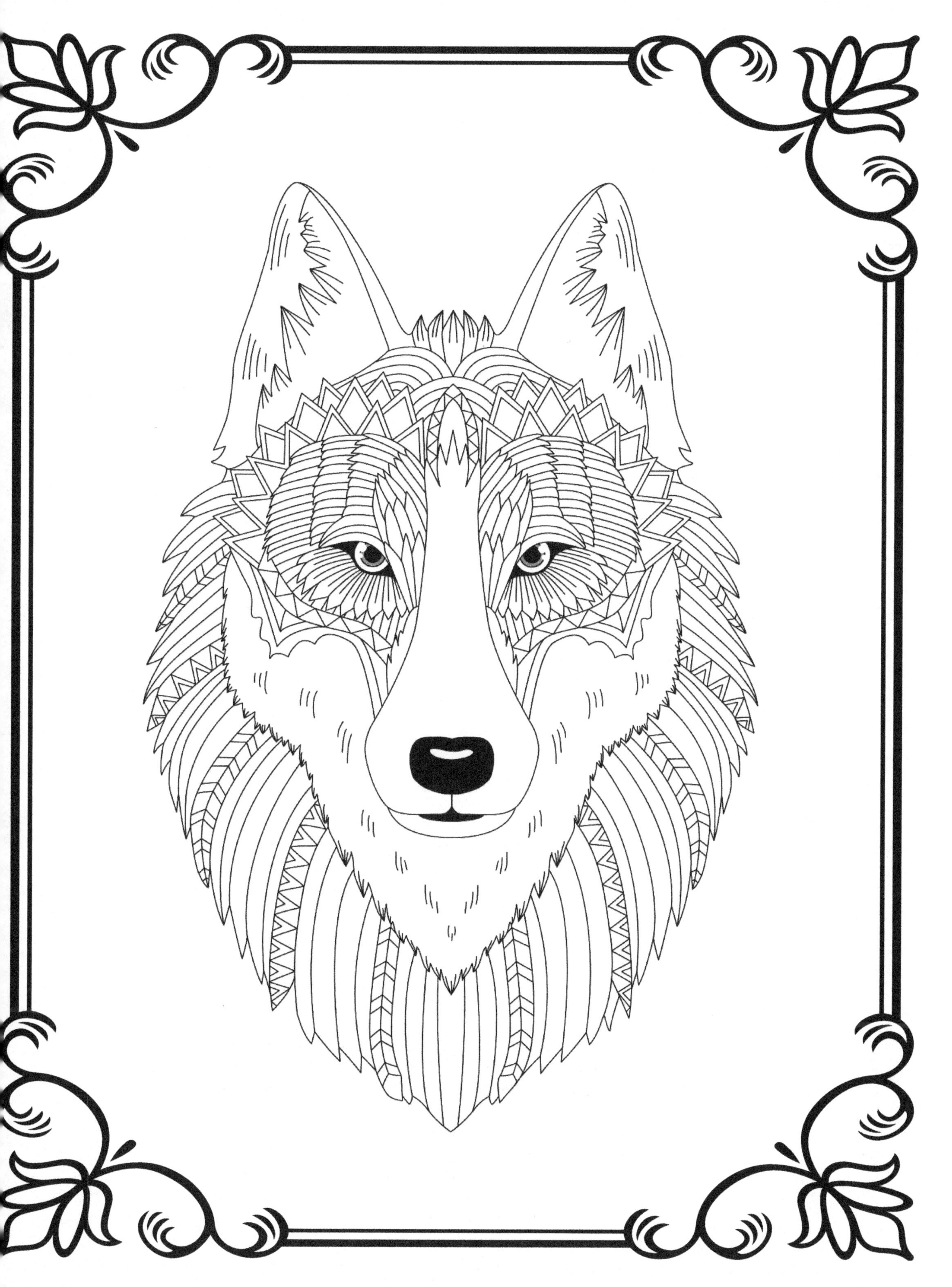

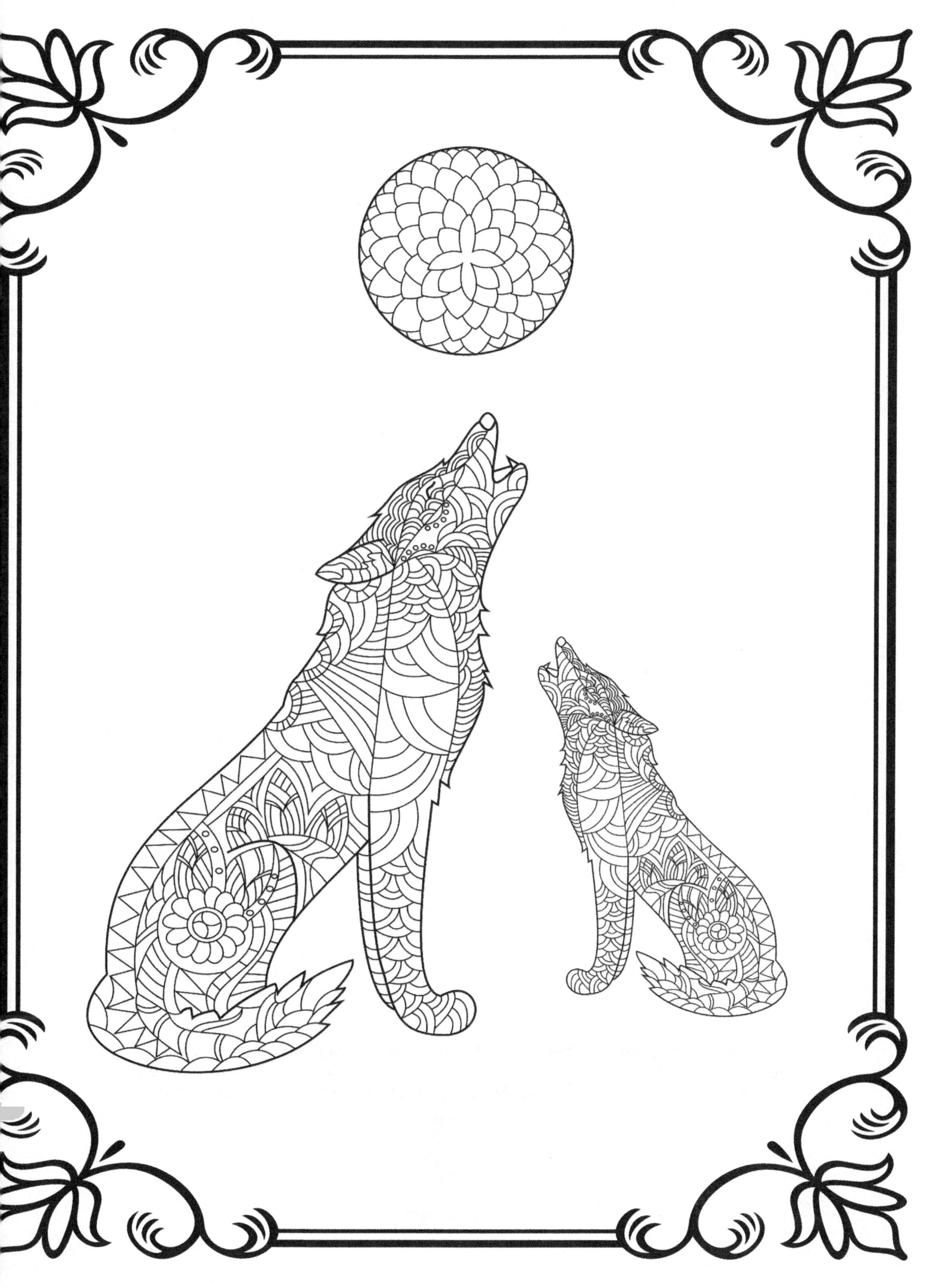

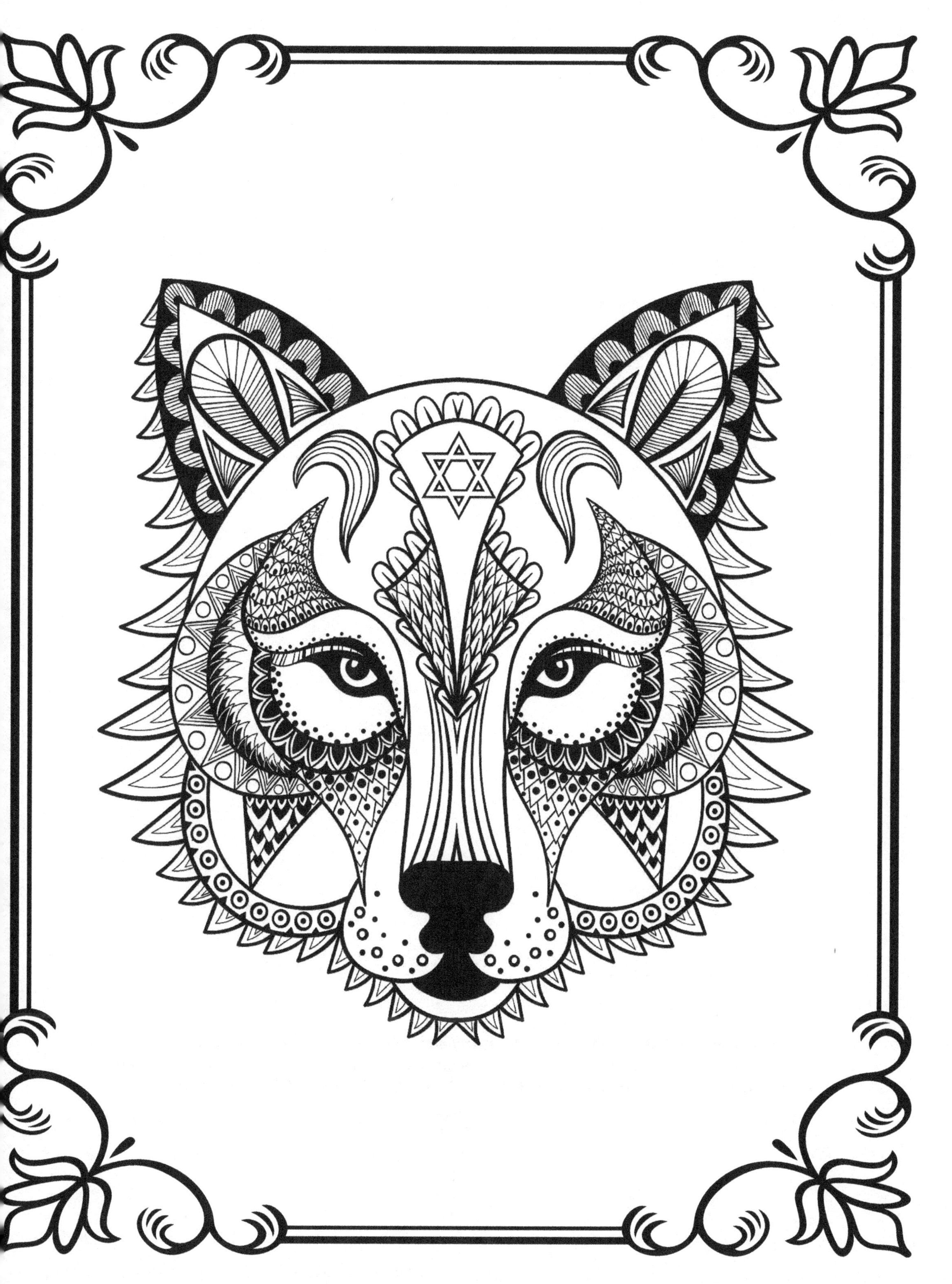

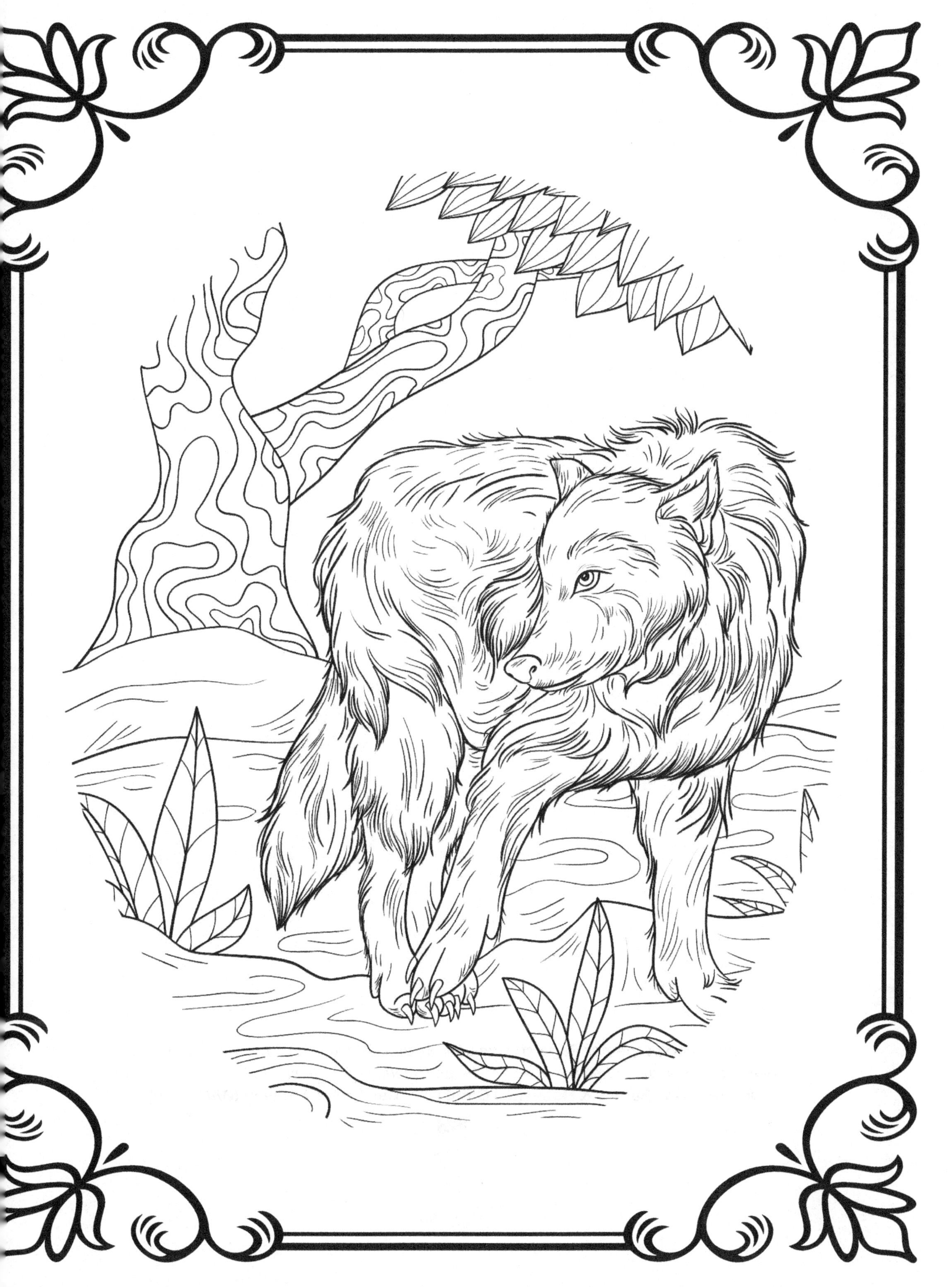

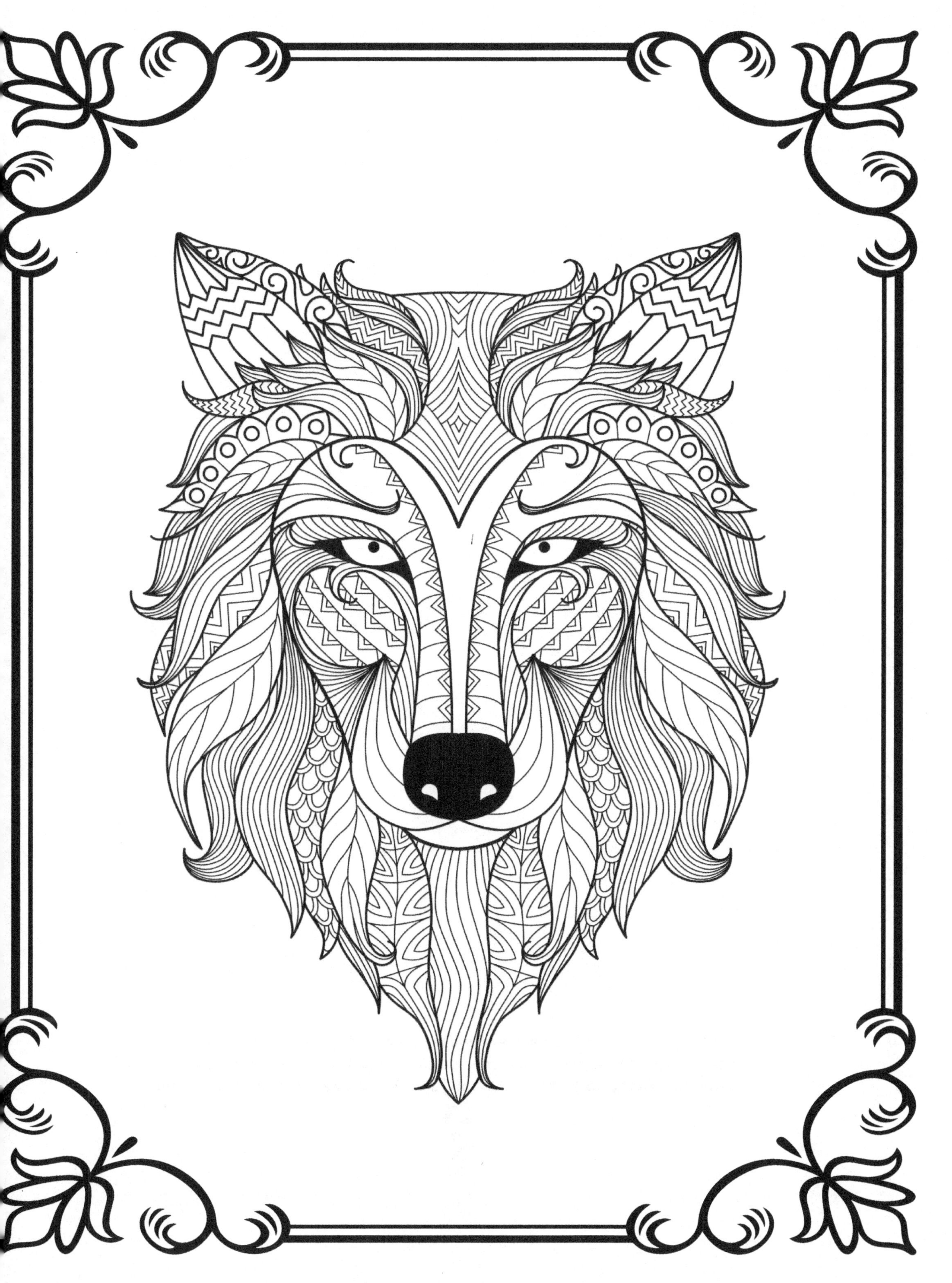

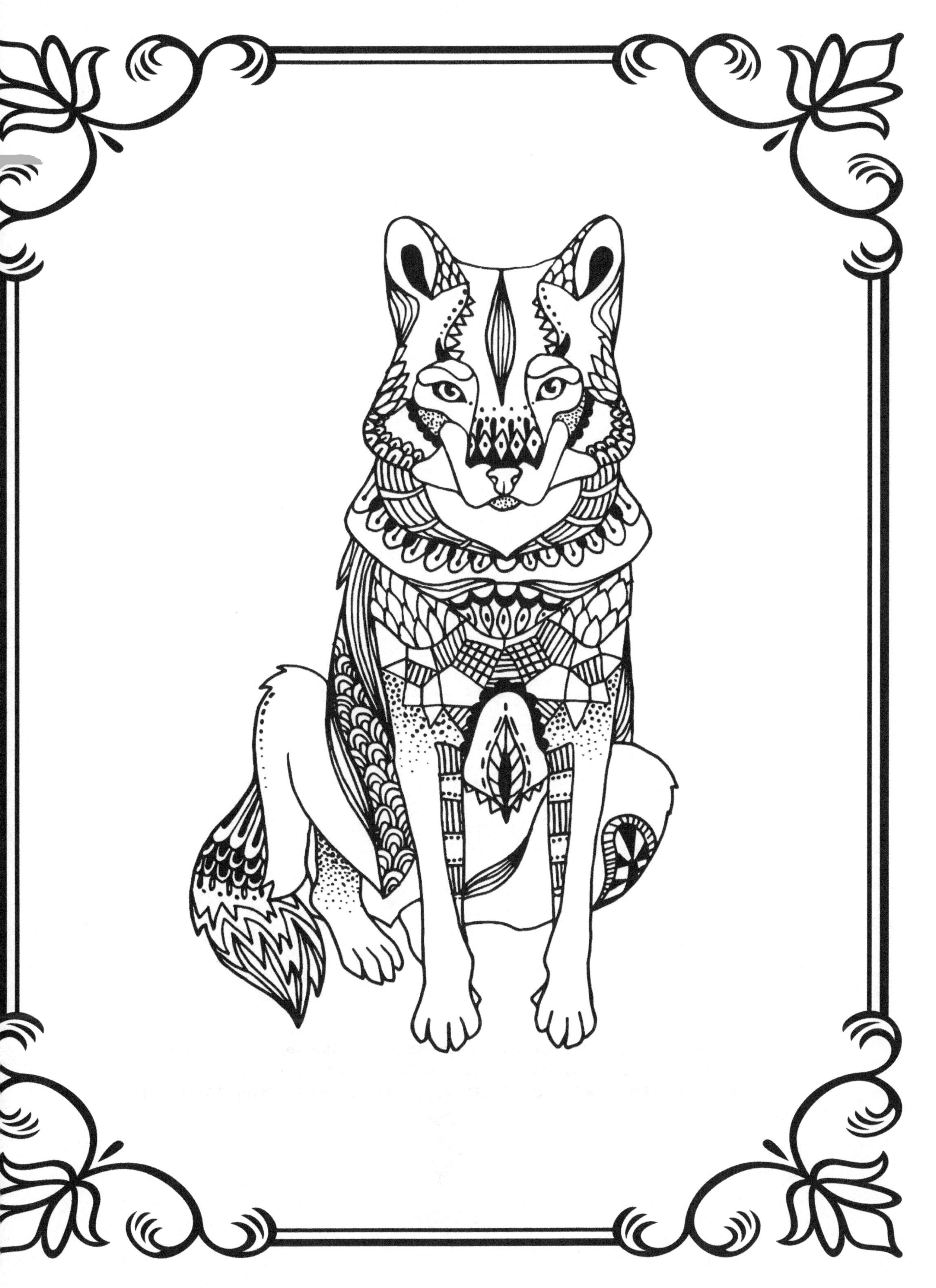

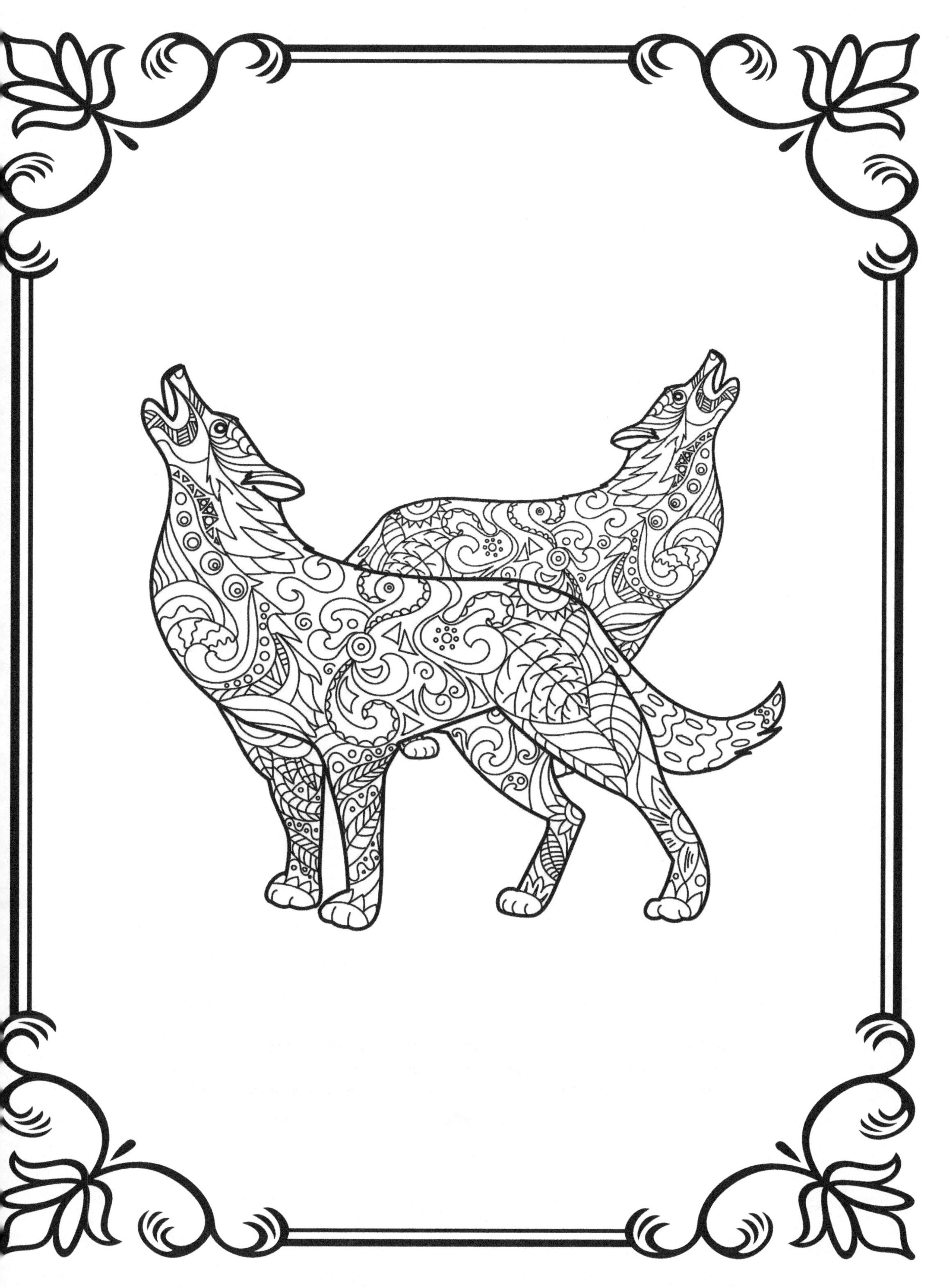

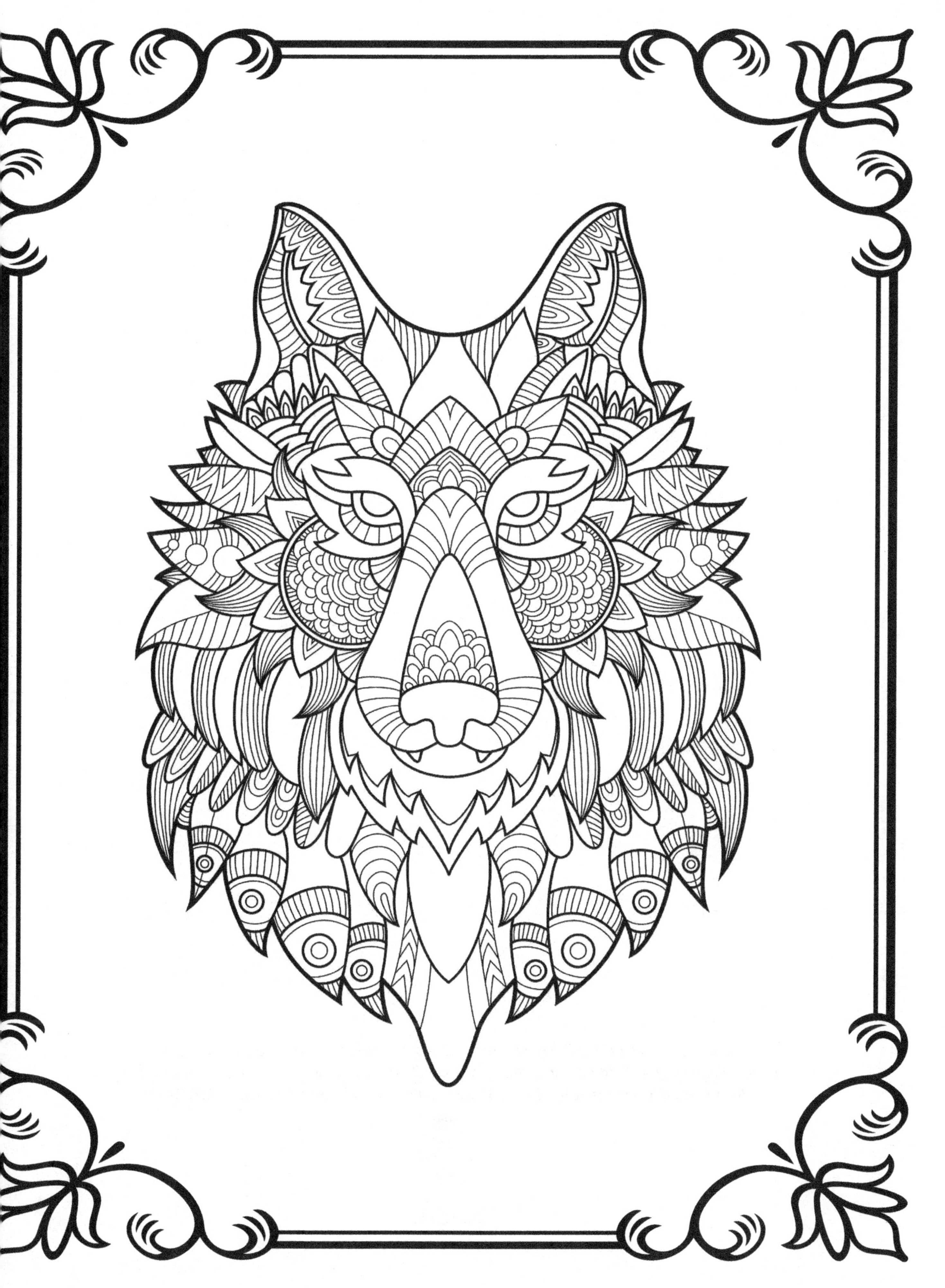

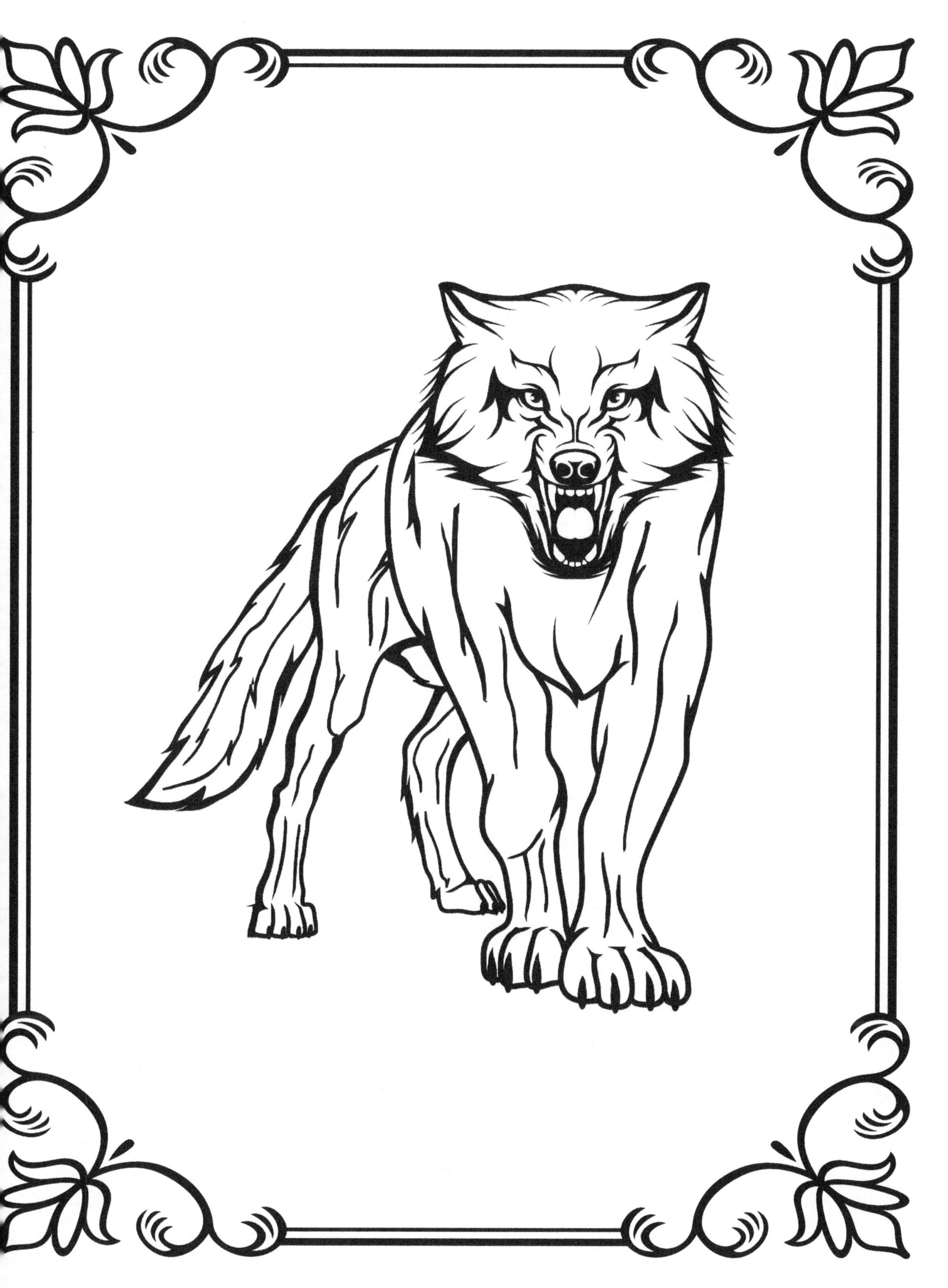

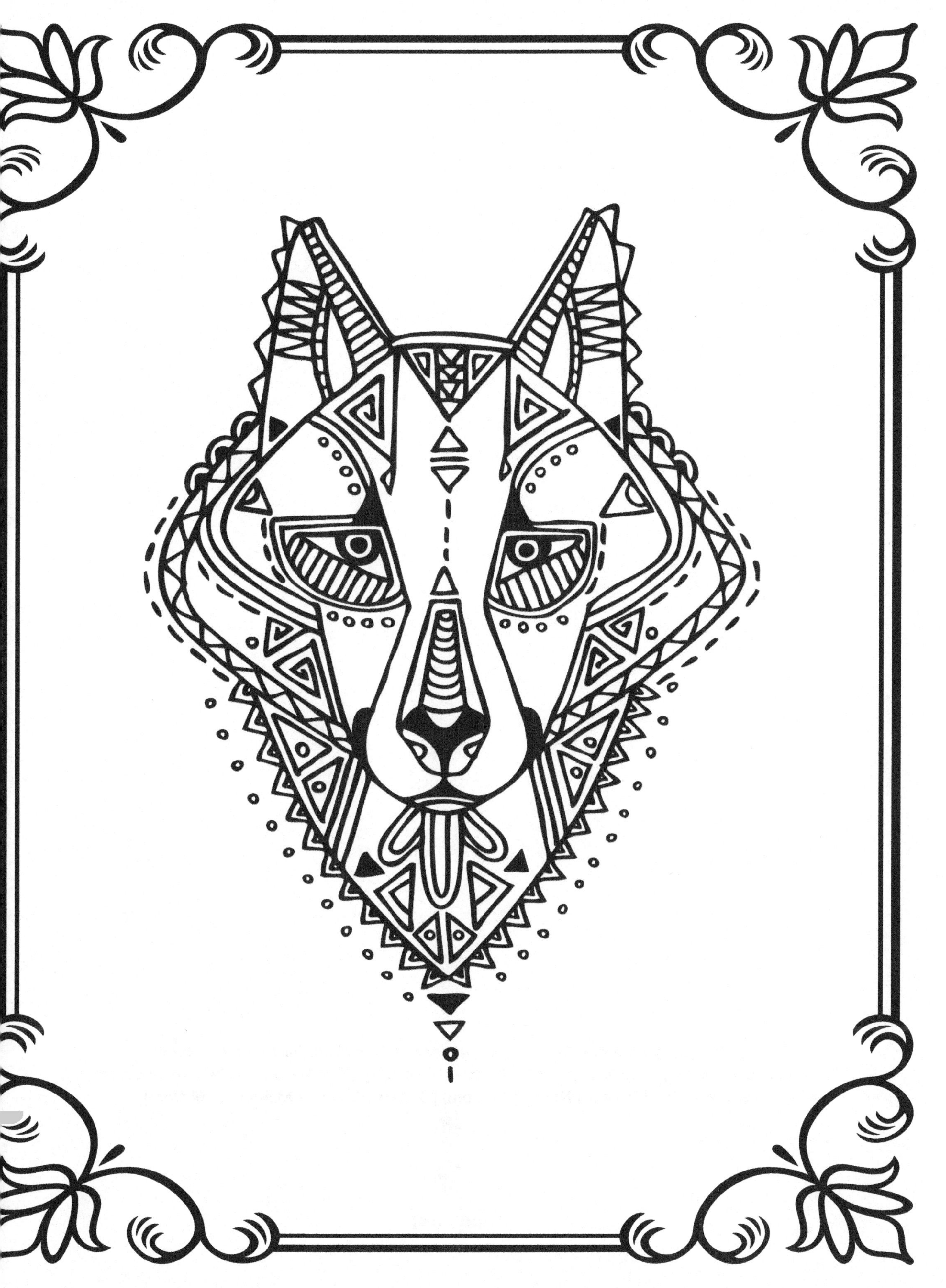

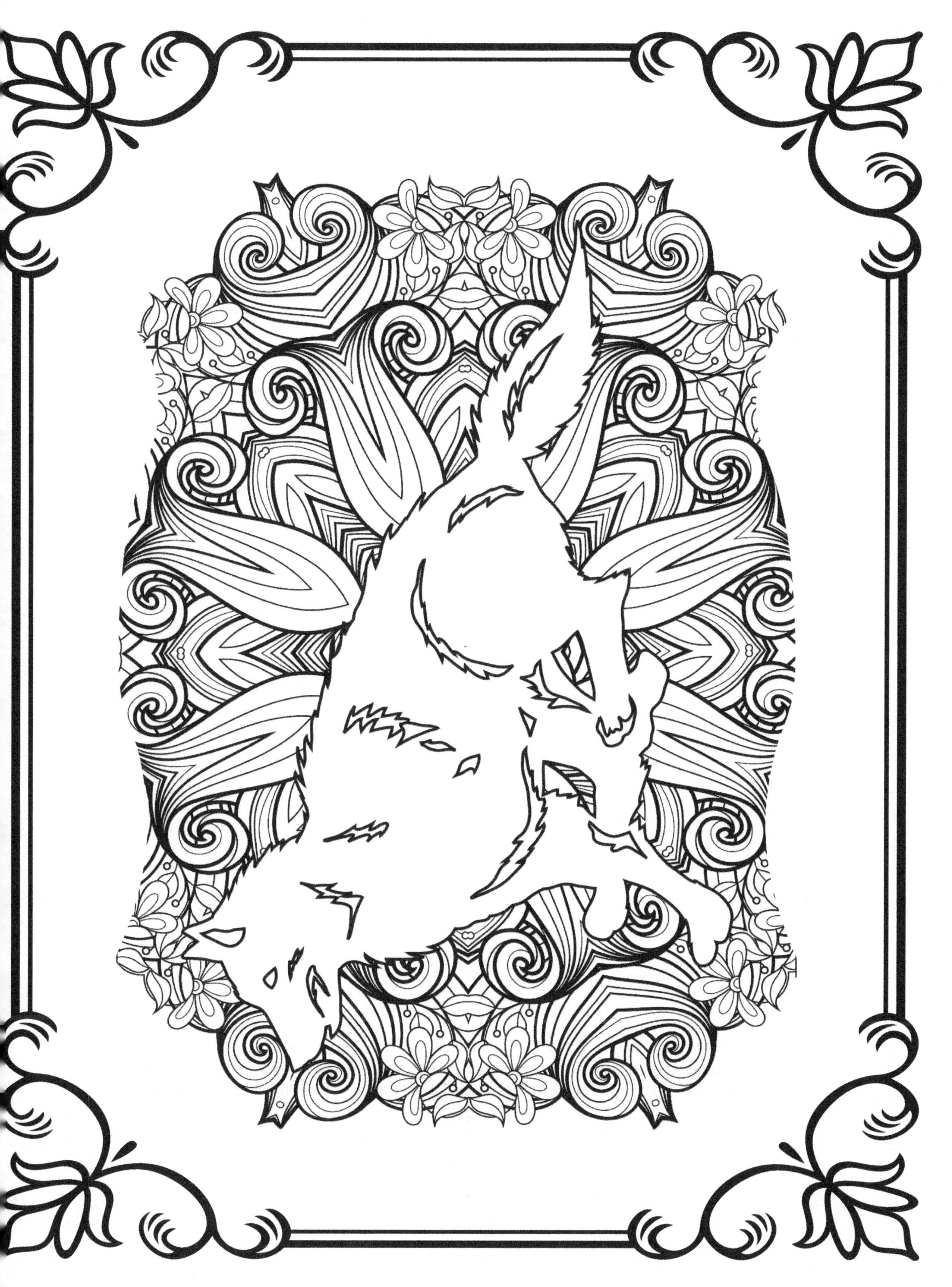

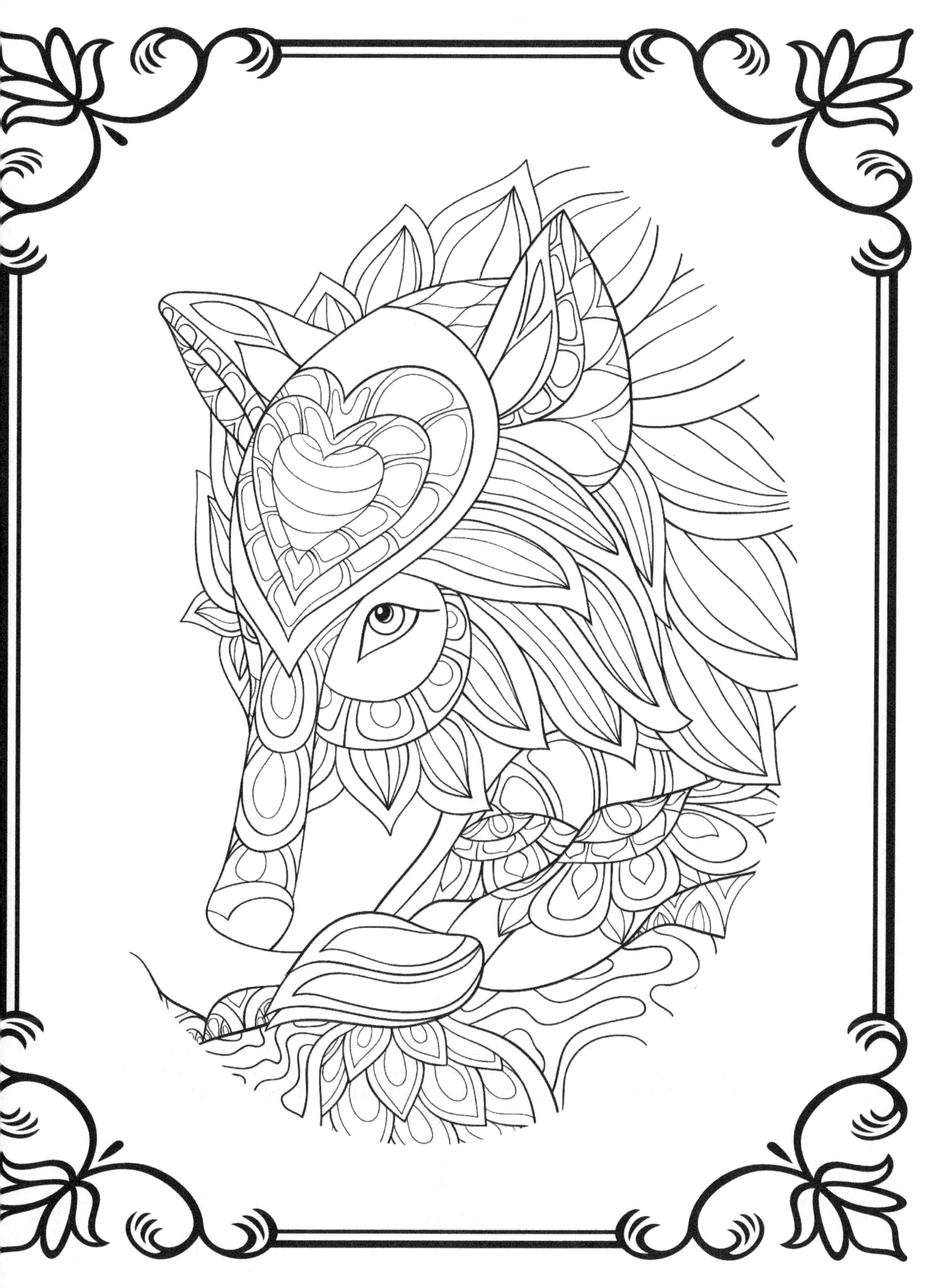

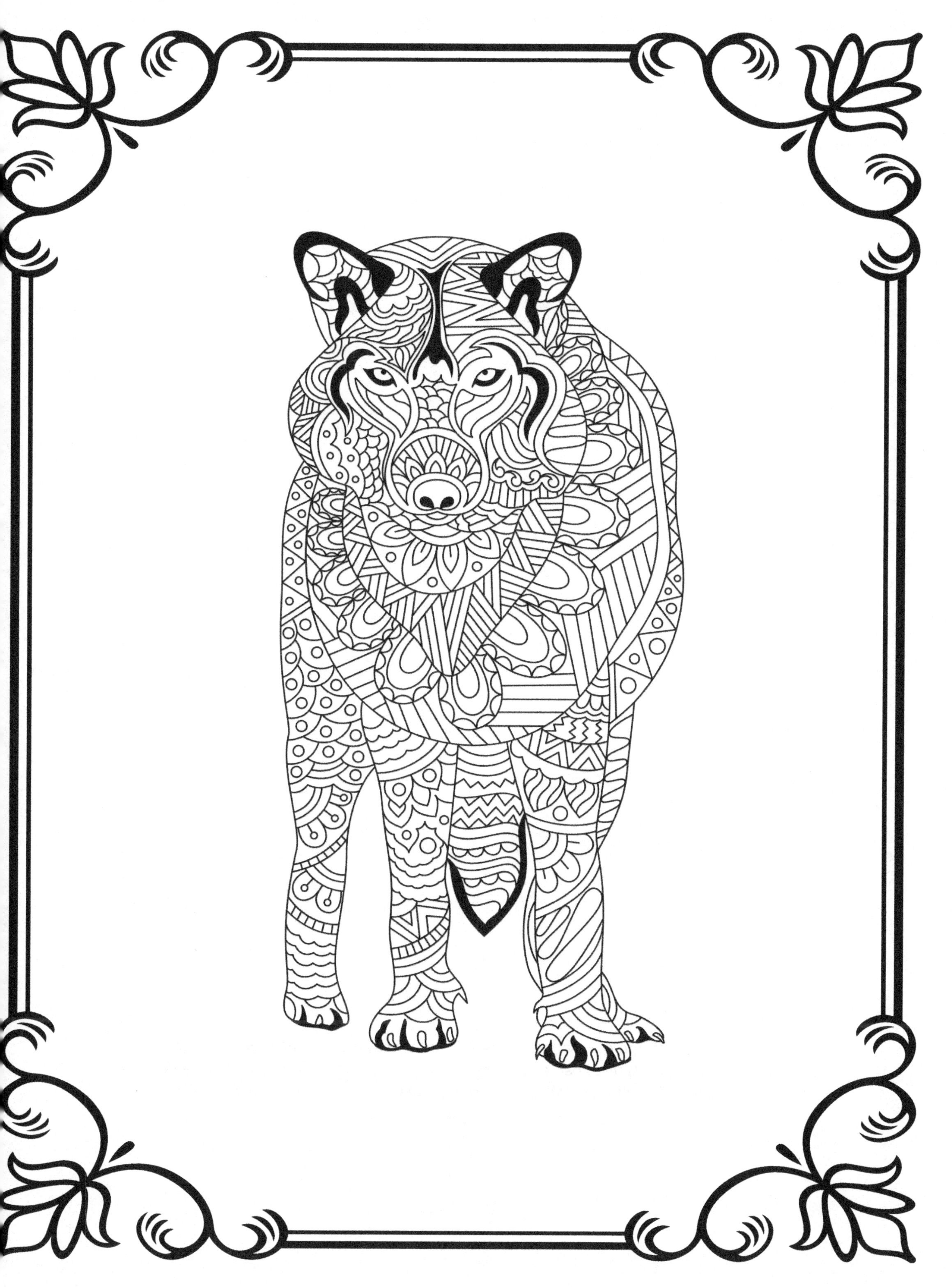

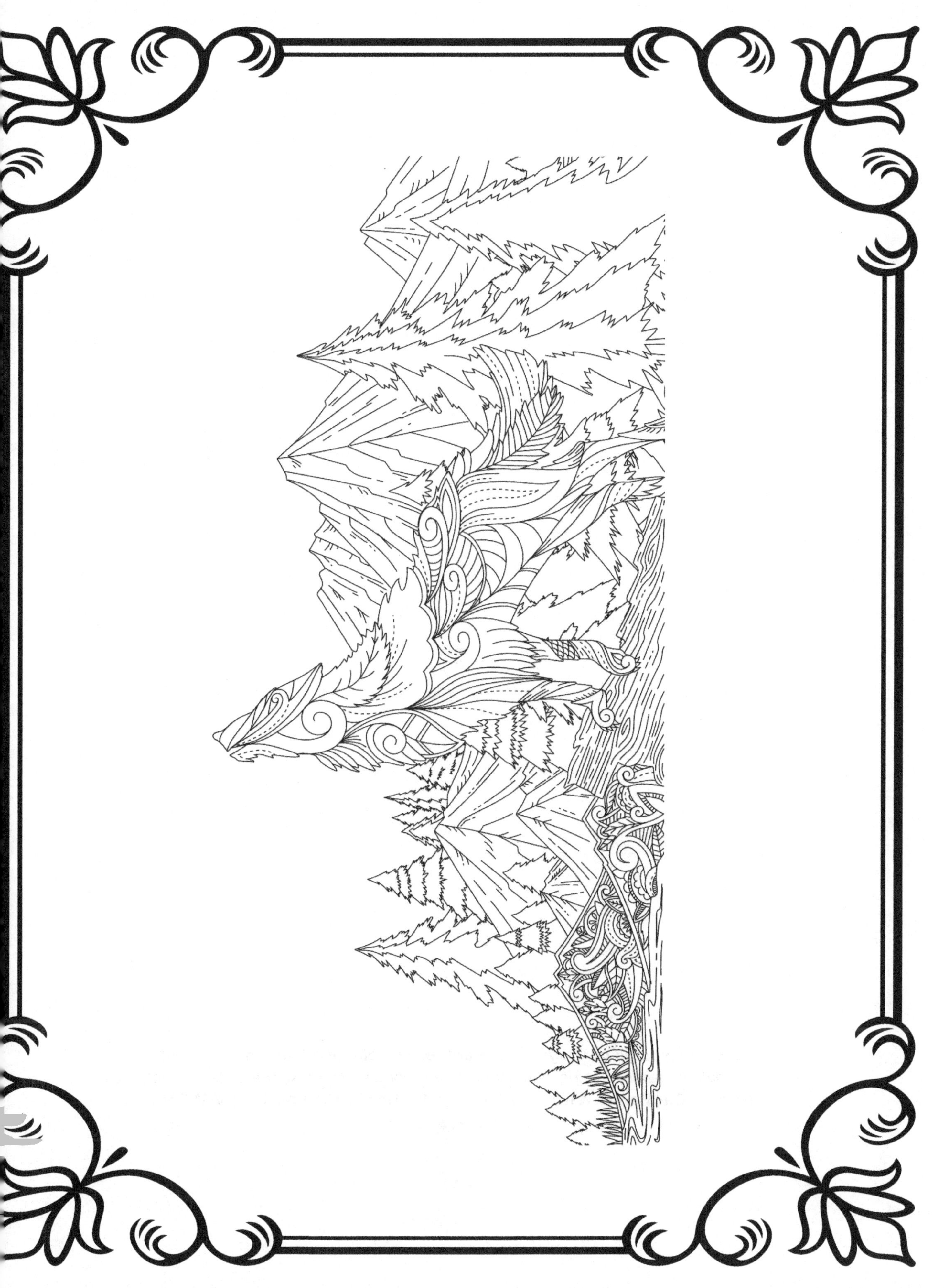

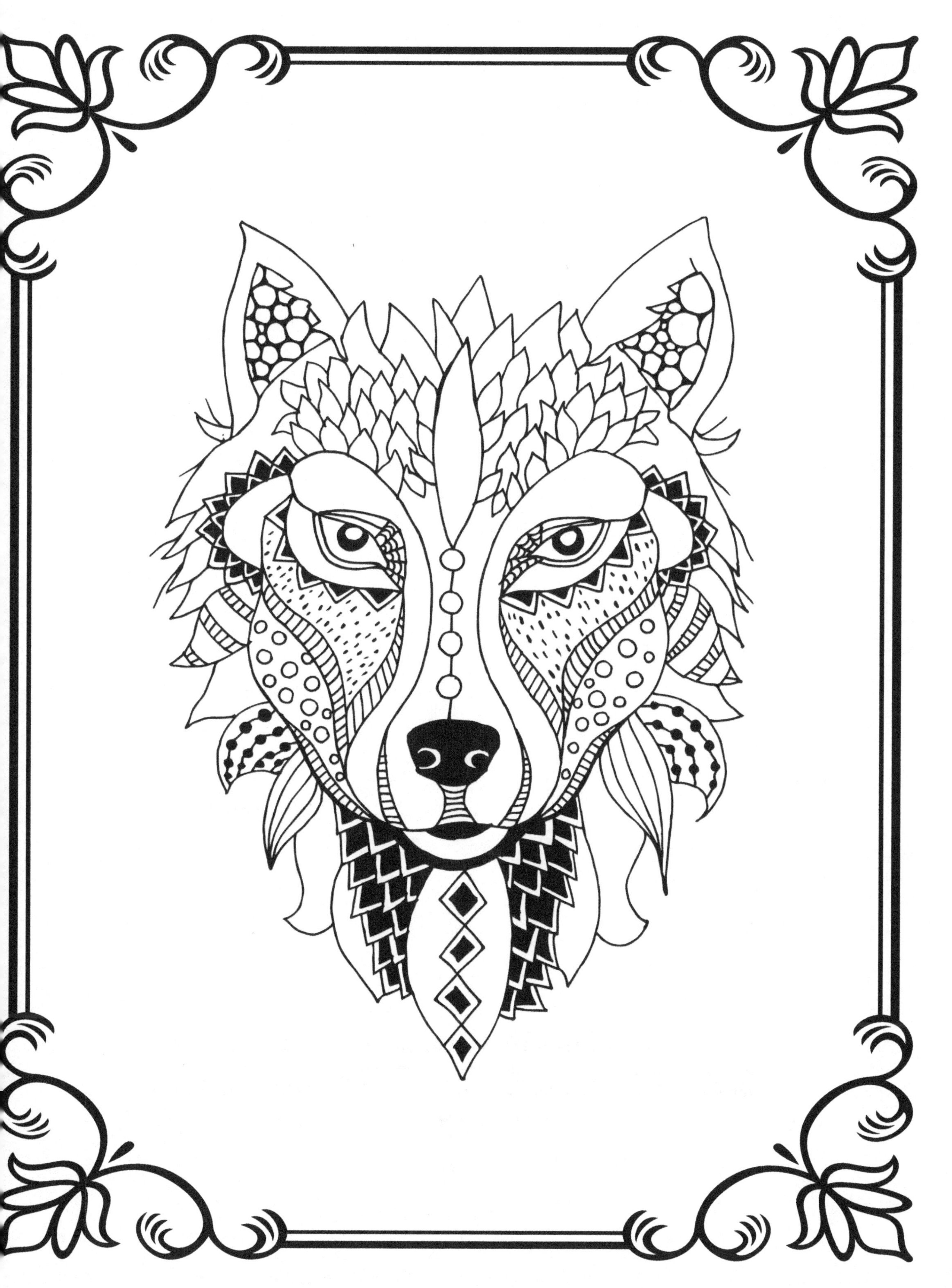

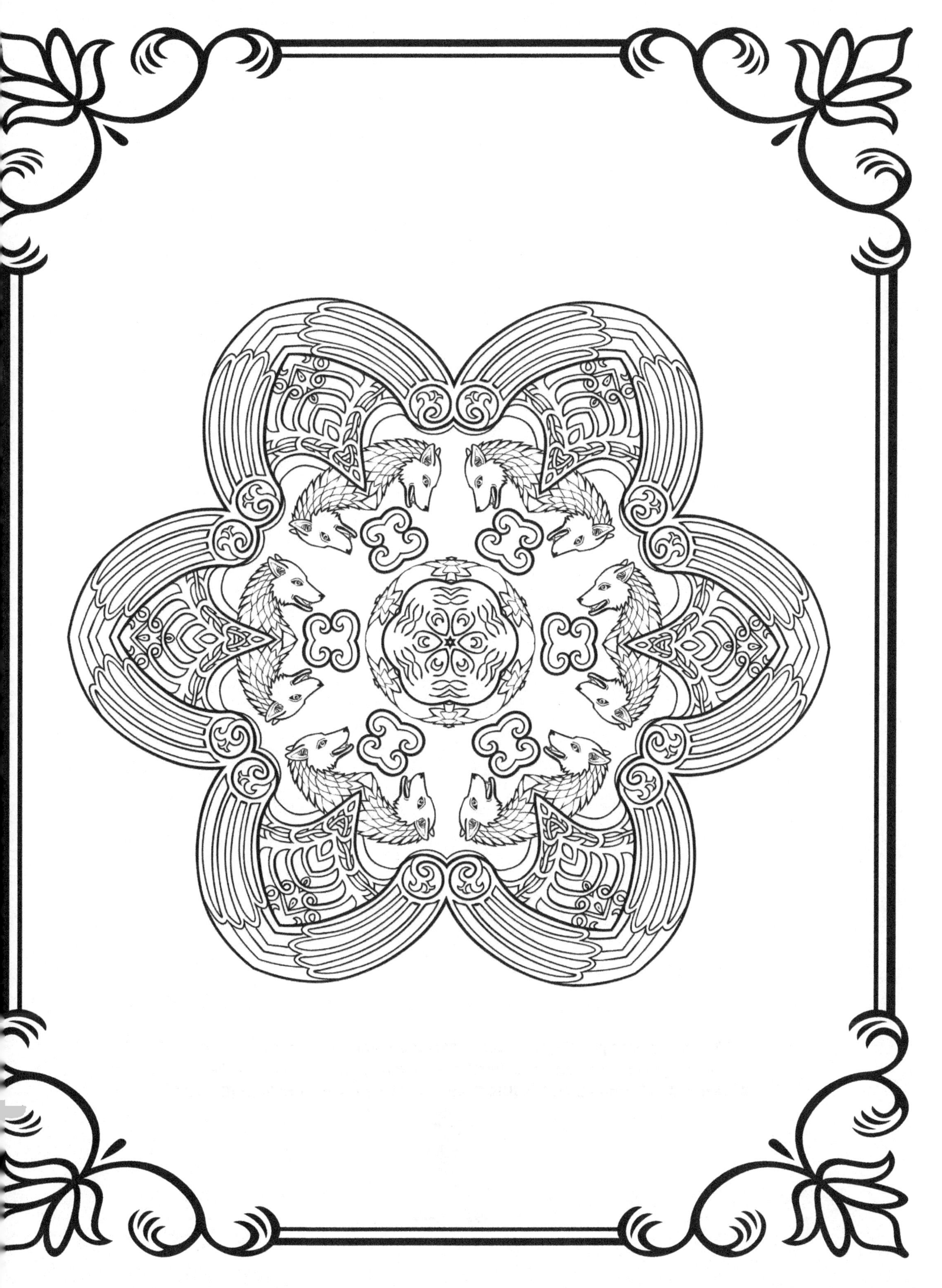

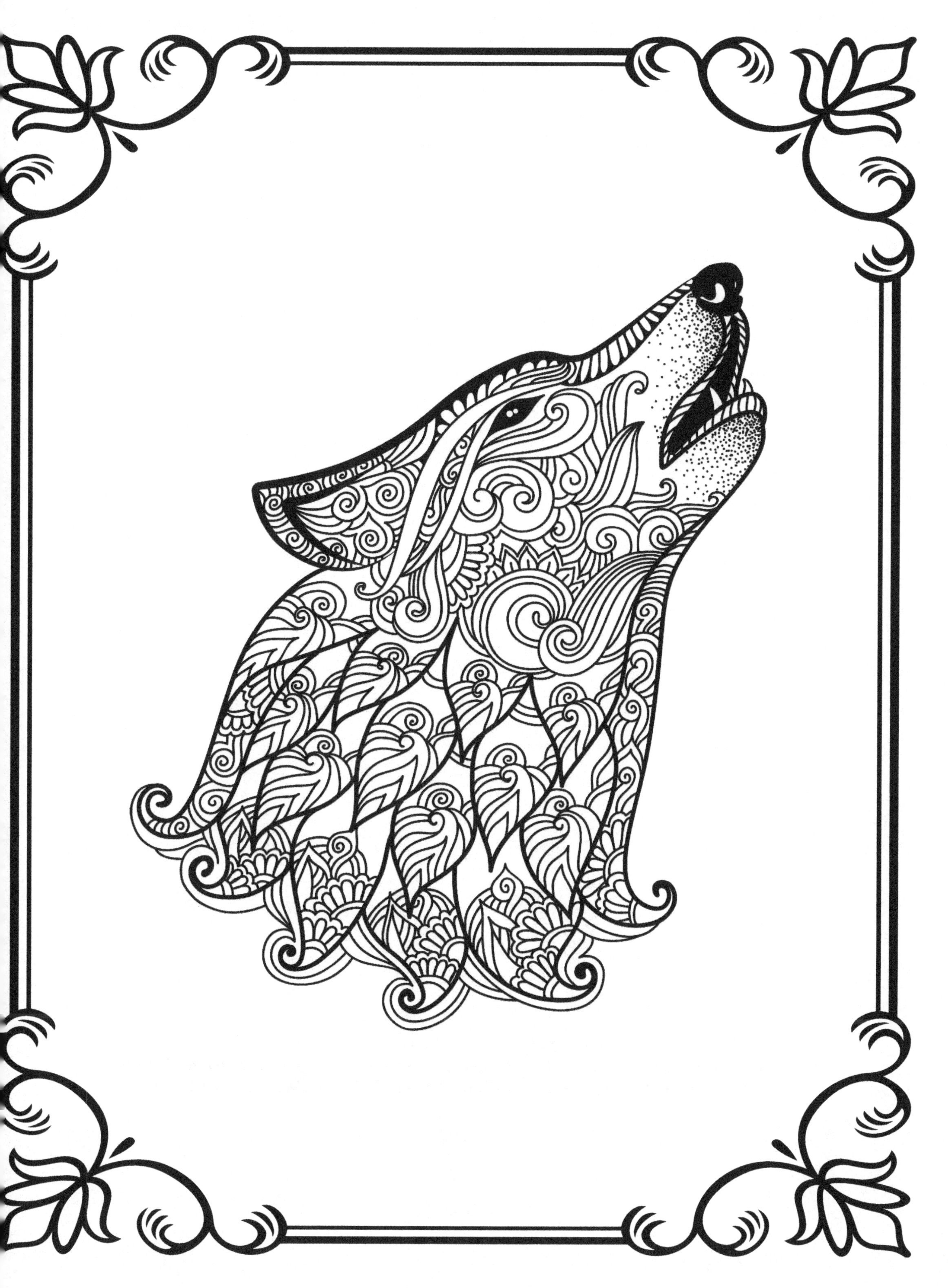

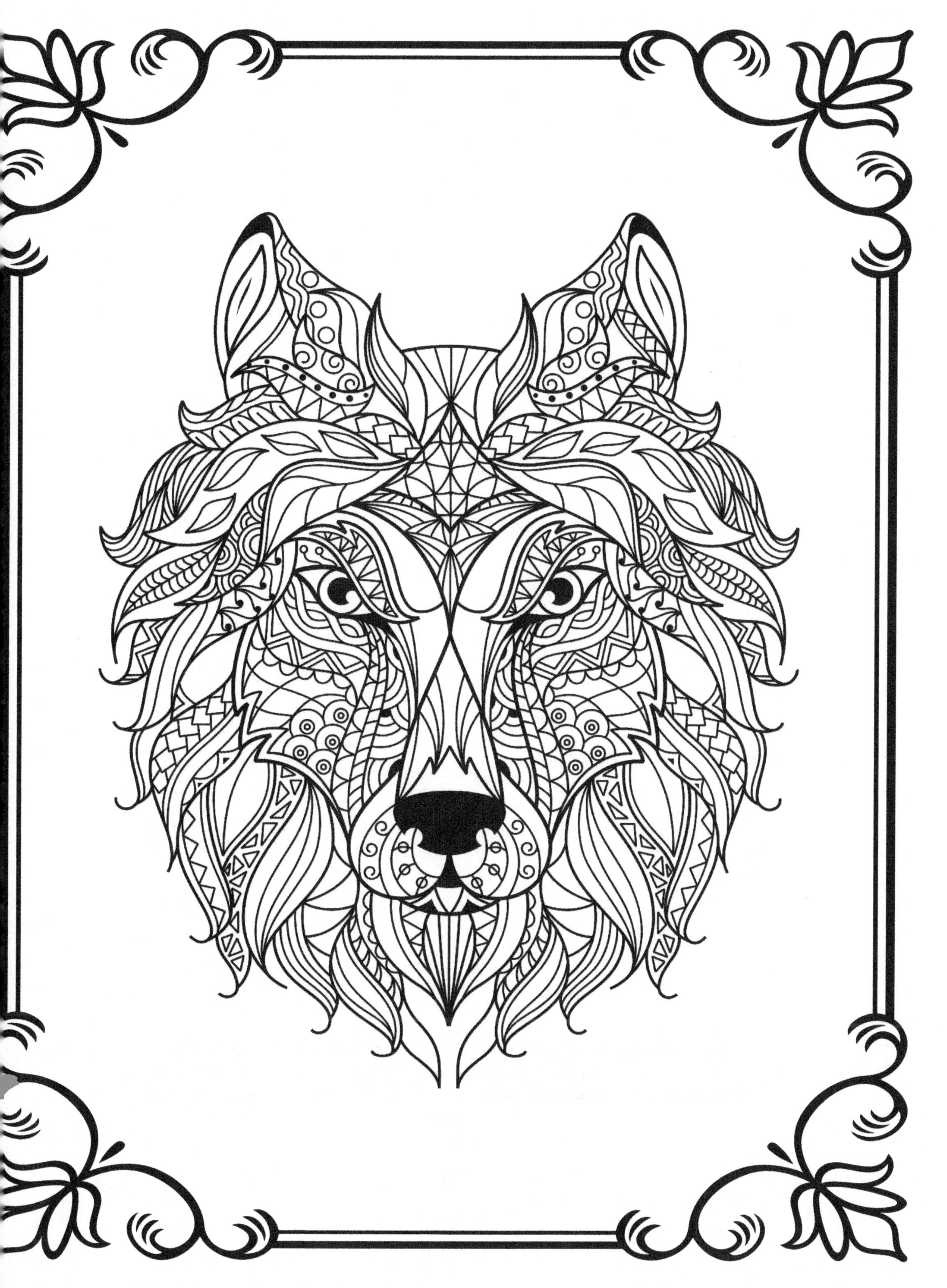

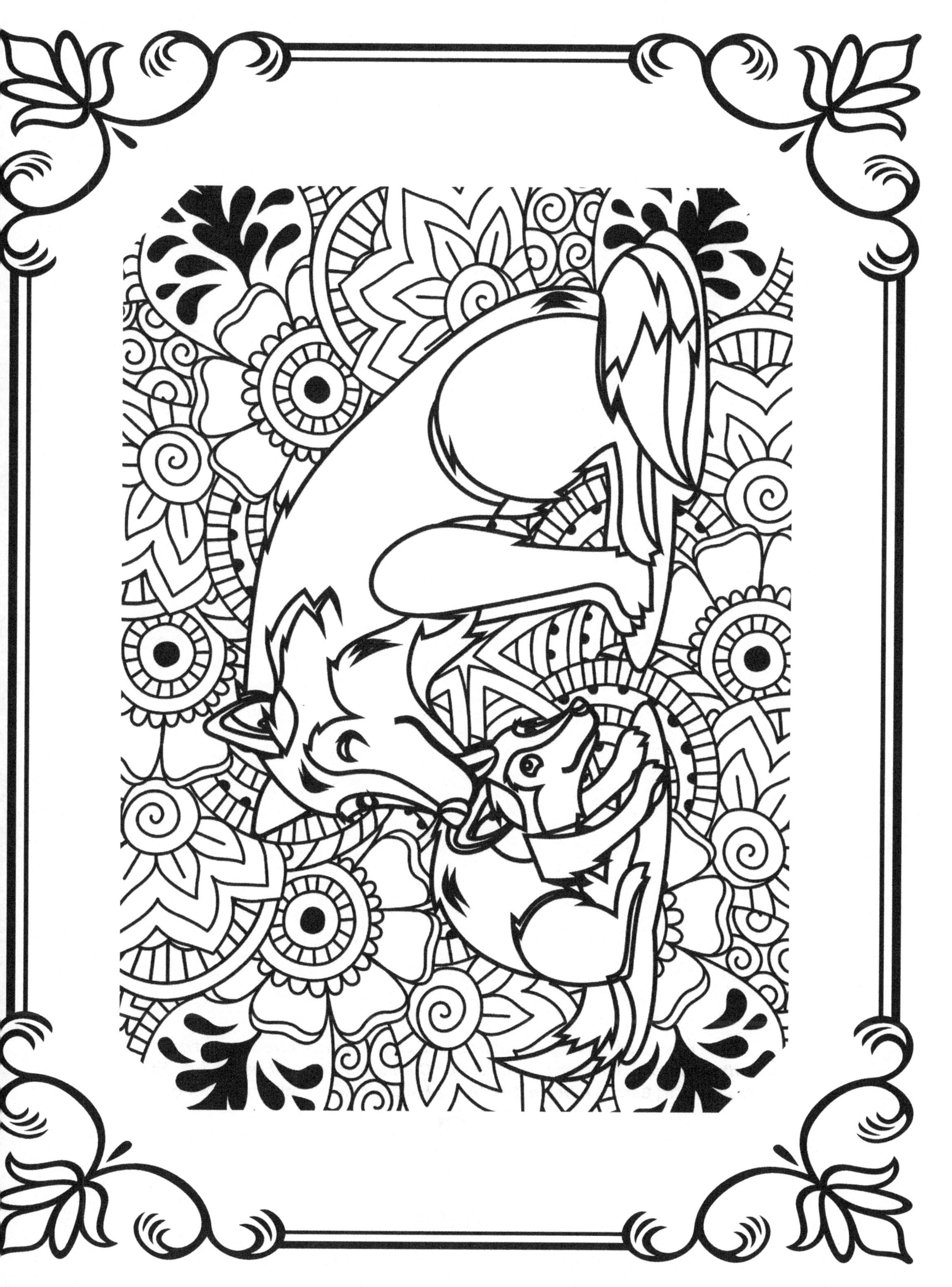

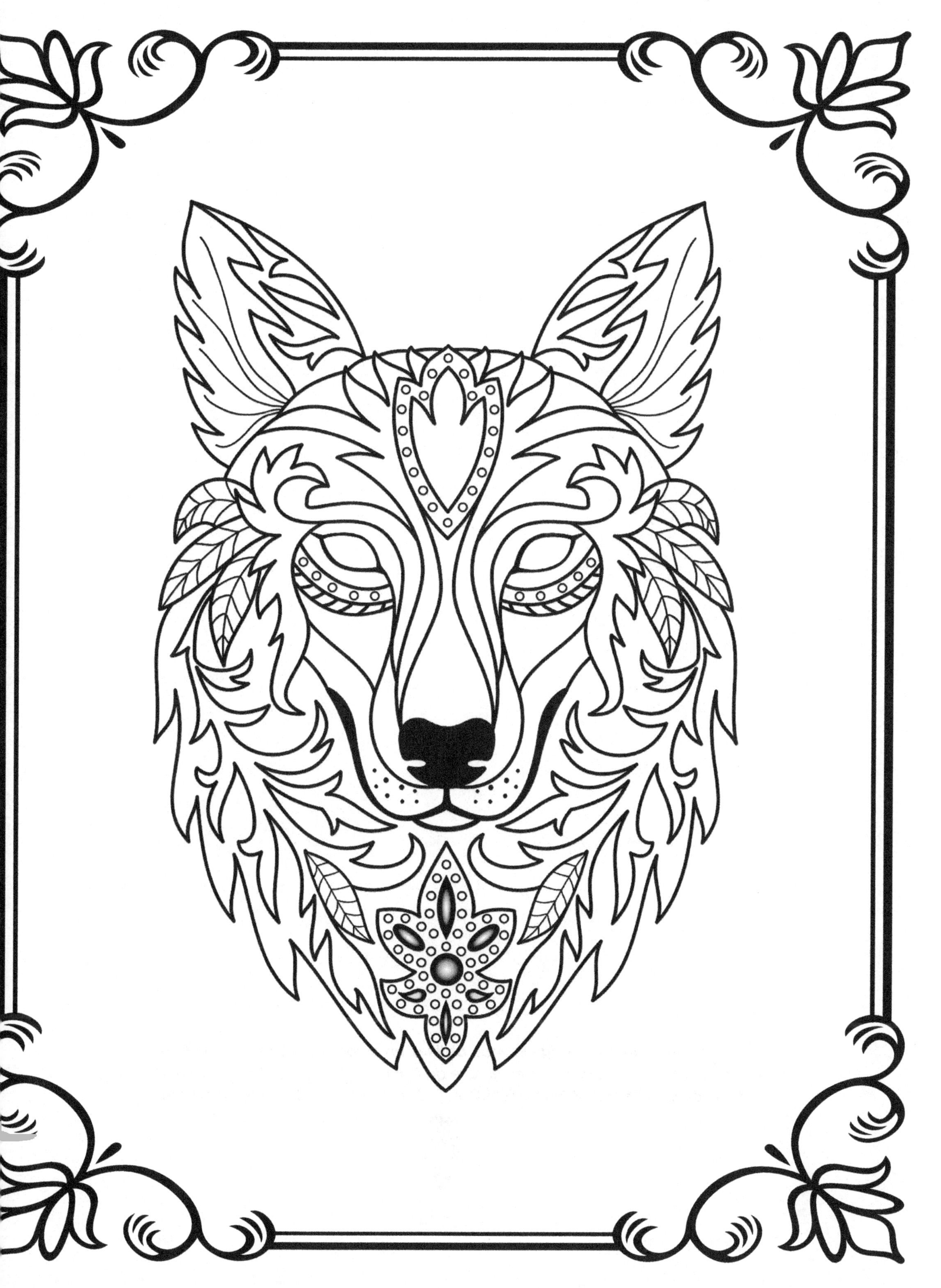

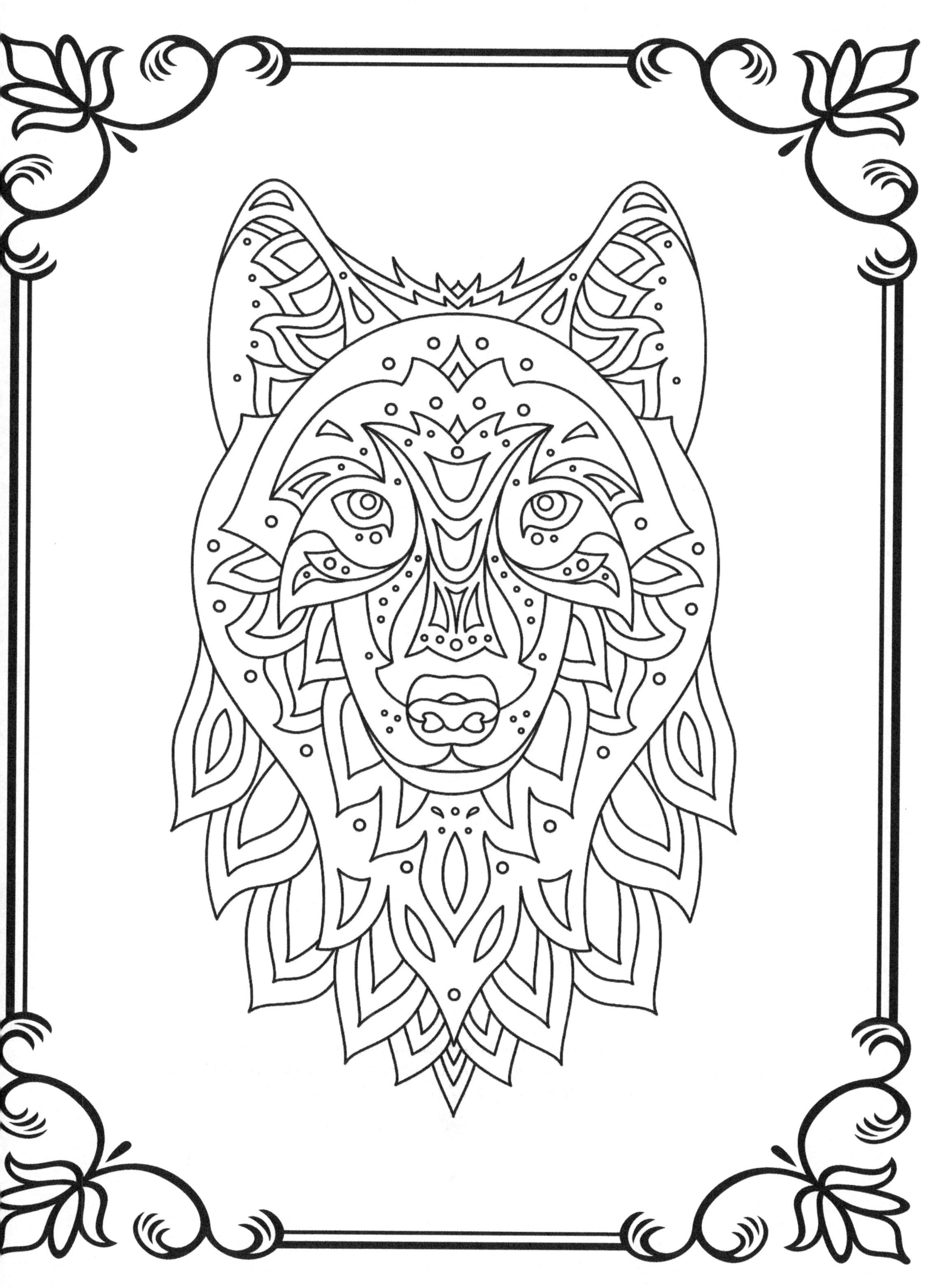

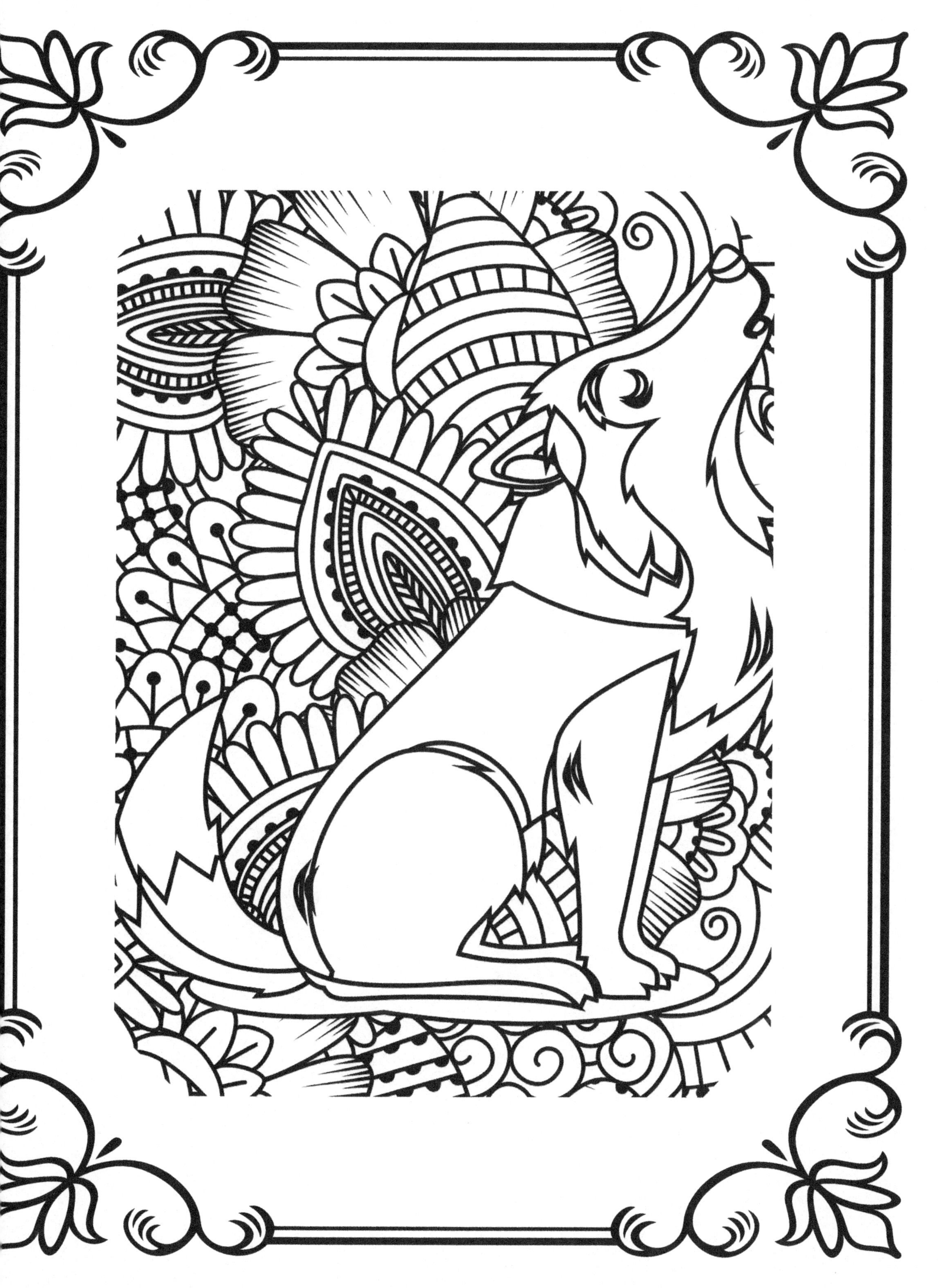

Made in the USA
Monee, IL
07 July 2026

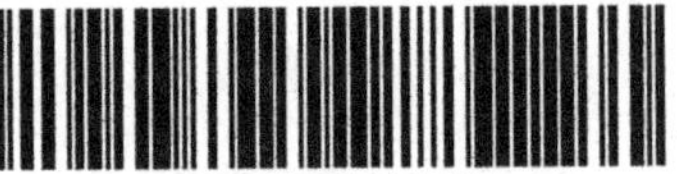